Personal Harmony

Christopher Walker

Order this book online at www.trafford.com/08-0635
or email orders@trafford.com

Most Trafford titles are also available at major online book retailers.

© Copyright 2008 Christopher John Walker.
All rights reserved. No part of this publication may be reproduced, stored in a retrieval system, or transmitted, in any form or by any means, electronic, mechanical, photocopying, recording, or otherwise, without the written prior permission of the author.

Edited by Simon Hillier
Cover Design/Artwork by Christian Blencke

Note for Librarians: A cataloguing record for this book is available from Library and Archives Canada at www.collectionscanada.ca/amicus/index-e.html

ISBN: 978-1-4251-7876-5

We at Trafford believe that it is the responsibility of us all, as both individuals and corporations, to make choices that are environmentally and socially sound. You, in turn, are supporting this responsible conduct each time you purchase a Trafford book, or make use of our publishing services. To find out how you are helping, please visit www.trafford.com/responsiblepublishing.html

Our mission is to efficiently provide the world's finest, most comprehensive book publishing service, enabling every author to experience success. To find out how to publish your book, your way, and have it available worldwide, visit us online at www.trafford.com/10510

www.trafford.com

North America & international
toll-free: 1 888 232 4444 (USA & Canada)
phone: 250 383 6864 • fax: 250 383 6804 • email: info@trafford.com

The United Kingdom & Europe
phone: +44 (0)1865 722 113 • local rate: 0845 230 9601
facsimile: +44 (0)1865 722 868 • email: info.uk@trafford.com

10 9 8 7 6 5 4 3

We consider our environment, we print on post-consumer recycled paper.

Dedication

I dedicate this book to a bloke I hardly knew who inspired me just by enjoying his life.

I raced a surf ski in the life saving carnivals in Australia. Sometimes the waves were 20 feet high, and to crash the ski was an amazingly dangerous thing. But it happened nearly every time, because so many of us were going down the waves thinking, "What happens if I crash?" One day, I was out in huge waves with an old guy, a veteran with the oldest wooden ski. As the biggest wave of the day rose behind us, twenty-five foot like a building, I watched this old guy, I saw the look on his face, and he was just like a child. He looked 15 years old, his smile could have lit a city, his hooting and hollering was so enthusiastic, he was having a ball. Instead of holding back, thinking, "What happens if..." he just threw his whole heart and soul into that wave and had the time of his life. I just fell in love with his exuberance, and thought that anybody who puts so much into anything they do is going to attract a crowd. He said to me later, "One great thing about age, there's less to go that there was, you know if you die, you may as well die with a smile on your dial, having a ball, doing it all."

"Do you know what astonishes me most in the world? The inability of force to create anything. In the long run, the sword is always beaten by the spirit."

Napoleon Bonaparte

Dear Friend,

Your True Nature is that part of you that is above conditioning, reaction and confusion. It is pure. It is your real potential. To the degree that we can be honest with ourselves, cut the rhetoric and separate our emotions from our truth, is the degree to which we can live authentically and in peace with life.

The cost of separating ourselves from nature is being recognized. The human cost of separating people from what is true and natural within them is becoming unquestionable. Our respect for humanity as a global family means we are returning to respect nature. This is inseparable from the quality of the environment we live in, both internal to ourselves and external in the world at large.

Knowing yourself, your True Nature, is a great contribution to this quest for a better life and a better world. This work invites you to look beyond the conditioning of your culture, your corporation and your family to find what is REAL within you. It invites you to explore your True Nature.

Throughout history those people who have come to understand what is natural within them have flourished in the long term. Your True Nature – is that part of you that is above conditioning, reaction and confusion. We call it inspiration. It is pure. It is your real potential. The degree to which we can be honest with ourselves, and find this reality, is the degree to which we can be in tune with nature and therefore be at our best.

With Spirit

Christopher Walker

"I want nothing
need nothing
therefore
I have everything"

Content

Introduction

Many years ago people were in tune with nature. Nature's harmony and human happiness were considered as one. They observed that what happened outside of us, was already happening within. But now, with time and technology, we have lost touch with this awareness. As our culture evolves into this current era, we suffer the separation from having worked with the land, understanding nature's rhythm and a dependency on nature for her sustenance. As we modernize, we have moved away from that harmony. The outer world has risen and taken precedence in our life, we look for solutions instead of awareness. We can all benefit from a more honest and deeper approach to life. If we can re connect with the harmony of nature, while remaining a part of the evolution of humanity, we will be able to celebrate both worlds, inner and outer harmony.

Nature is the keeper of sacred law and for the benefit of your life, to live in harmony, those laws can be yours. The forest, the ocean, the sky, species, rocks, plants, animals and insects all have a voice. It requires silence and wisdom to hear it and it is here that this specific learning will impact your lifestyle; It will help you create harmony in your work, stimulate changes in your environment, direct the exercises you do and help create the depth and silence that sustains harmony within you.

Harmony with nature comes from within. Your life and work can become in tune with nature. Nature is surrounding you every moment and you can witness her beauty in every breath. It can heal you, help you grow, inspire you, hold you when you are sick and, most importantly, guide you into a future of contentment.

The appetite for harmony in life is born within every human heart. The paths to it vary widely but the laws of nature are the most universal path. They do not discriminate with wealth, age, religion, culture or attitude; they are transparent. They don't compete with religion, culture or anything. They just stand as a testimony to the order that lies beneath. Order is the awareness of a great mystery. The person who knows this mystery understands the beauty of life.

Chapter 1. Personal Harmony
Finding your True Nature

"I would rather have the whole world against me, than my own Soul."

Christopher Walker

For a business executive, life may be harmonious if the cash is flowing, clients are happy and the future is rosy. Ask a devout Buddhist and of course they will define harmony as peace and non-violent action. Ask a fundamentalist terrorist and the answer might be quite violent, they may even define harmony as the elimination of a whole race of humanity, but that is not the true harmony humanity seeks.

The path to personal harmony is a deep, personal journey and building a harmonious future is the hidden quest of most humanity. All human eyes are turned to the future. Therefore the desire for personal harmony becomes our most discrete motive for existence.

This is a path beyond self-obsession. We cannot immunize our own personal harmony from the greater harmony of the world. Our safety and freedom hinges on contribution and compassion for others, making sure others have human rights and that global affairs are part of our responsibility. Global affairs are an integral part of our personal search; we must contribute in order to feel "the touch of our Soul". Our journey toward personal harmony and the depth of our contribution to the global affairs of the world is one in the same topic. Our quest for harmony and our duty of care for others, including humanitarian rights of the world are inextricably linked. But first, we get our own house in order.

The one who finds personal harmony does not do so, as most think, by quenching their material thirst. Nothing of the sense ever satisfied the Soul. So the appetite that drives our external life and all it's trimmings is vastly different to the higher calling of the Soul, which is one of contribution: it comes from within.

The inner world gains its harmony by attunement. The laws for this inner attunement are written for us. They are the Laws of Nature, the Ancient Mysteries and these can be found simply by entering the forest, the beach, the garden and finding your attunement. The nature of all existence has stamped upon it the keynotes of the harmony of life. Nature holds the key and she is there, everywhere, waiting for you to discover her, all you need is the code that is here in this book. Nature has the ability to free your mind to see order and beauty and bring harmony to your heart. When our expectations and thinking match the rhythm of natural law, we begin to work in harmony with all existence and with this, our world, and the world around us will change.

How do I know if I am living in harmony or not?

Most people see personal harmony as a difficult attainment. It's not. It is neither difficult nor an attainment. Wherever it is that you are, you are in fact already harmonious, you just may not know it. Nothing new is to be added and nothing is to be discarded; you are as perfect as possible, RIGHT NOW. It is not that you are going to be perfect sometime in the future; it is not that you have to do something arduous to be yourself. It is not the journey to some other point somewhere else; you are not going somewhere else. You are already there. That which is to be obtained is already attained. This idea must go deep, only then will you be able to understand why such simple techniques can help.

You just have to become more of what you were meant to become. Born as a seed, your true nature is revealed when you have flowered. You have come to complete growth, an inner growth, to the inner end. Now this will contradict the ideal that we must aspire to be the best we can or that we must continually evolve in order to find ourselves. In this concept of finding your "True Nature" you aspire to be complete. That means totally content, comfortable with who you are, inspired by a purpose larger than ourselves and connected to the vitality of life. At this point we can totally surrender and become what is described as living our True Nature.

Whatever this means, the ultimate experience is to be in total contentment, to want absolutely nothing. To desire nothing. To be totally content with yourself. Then there is nothing lacking; there is no desire, no movement. And then from this place all actions are taken with purity. Then whatever you touch, whatever you are doing or not doing -- even just existing -- is a peak experience. You are alive and that is enough. Then growth can occur in harmony with nature.

If you are not perfect already then there is no possibility, there is no way that you can become perfect. The whole situation is totally the opposite of searching for identity; you are already that which you want to attain. That is why simple techniques can help. It is not an attainment, but the discovery. It is hidden, and it is hidden in very, very, small things.

Personas are just like clothes. Your body is here, it is hidden in clothes. In the same way your inner truth is here, hidden in certain clothes. These clothes are your ego-personality. You can be buck naked right here and now, and in the same way you can be naked in your True Nature right here and now also. But if you do not know what clothes are covering your true nature, it is impossible to take them off. If you do not know how you are hidden in those clothes, you will not know how to be naked. We have been in these ego clothes for so long, covering our true inspired nature for years and years and years, so we have even forgotten that we are in clothes -- we become so identified with our ideas, our beliefs and our achievements, that we don't even recognize them as clothes. You might think these things; ideas, possessions, religions and relationships are you. And that is the only barrier to your inspired nature.

For example, you hear about some treasure, and you think you know where people have hidden it. And the grass has grown and trees have grown all around and then you have no way of understanding where that treasure is. The place doesn't look like it does on the map. Then you begin looking for it all over the place, you search high and low and you dig at all the ground and you become like a crazy person, going to retreats, hunting and hunting for the precious treasure. You know that you can be wealthy when you find it, but it is hidden in a place and now you can't remember where. And then one day when you finally give up searching, after all the ground has been completely uncovered you realize that the real treasure was not somewhere to be found. It was in your pocket.

It is the same with your True Nature; it is a hidden treasure. The more you search for it, the harder it gets to find. It cannot be in the future because the future, tomorrow, never comes. You are the treasure that you are looking for. Your judgments against yourself disguise the treasure. Your beliefs about what is good and bad about others and yourself are the clothes that cover the treasure. This treasure is your inner peace, your freedom, your joy, your contentment, your focus, and your concentration.

So, there is a certain relaxed calm that descends over a person who has found their True Nature. The inner power, the heart, gives a radiance; a constant showering of love and inspiration seems to come from them. There is a silent power surrounding them. When a person has found harmony within – it is a personal spirituality, they have become content with themselves and their energy becomes infectious. Just as negativity can be infectious so the positive energy of an inspired person can become infectious. We know this as leadership and radiance. But it is not leadership of the mind or intellect; it is leadership of the True Nature, the Soul, the human spirit.

Living truth – Three keys to Personal Harmony.

Living from personal harmony, means to find your centre. To hold that centre no matter whether you are thinking in the head or feeling in the heart, the centre stays strong. That means achieving great inspiration but still having a firm grip on reality, grounded. That centre is never missing.

For the centred person everything becomes sacred, beautiful, and whole. Whatever he or she is doing, no matter what it is, they focus their mind and take full mindfulness. Nothing is trivial. They will not say, "this is small and this is large." This is important and this is unimportant, no, for them everything holds the same weight. A self-actualized person, a balanced, centred person, feels in harmony with everything. You can feel it in their touch. The great doctors and healers of our time have been known for the power of their touch, the softness of the disposition and the power of the concentration.

A person who is centred is the same, no matter who they are with, or where they are. They have the same inner quality. When meeting a beggar they are not different from meeting a King. When on stage they are identical to offstage. When alone they are no different then when they are with friends. This is the mark of a person who has uncovered their True Nature; they are centred, completely natural. There is no need to pretend, there is no act to present. They practice between performances. Falsehood has no place in their life because the centre is the axis around which they live their life. This includes handling discomfort and pain. Can you imagine being centred enough to welcome pain with the same loving kindness as you welcome pleasure? This is real personal harmony.

The second key to personal harmony is that the person remains balanced. Their life is balance. They are never one-sided, they never make a stand, they are never righteous because they understand that everything in this world is built in duality and therefore to stand on one side or the other breeds imbalance. A person who is imbalanced will have significant swings of emotion from infatuation to resentment, elation to depression, and attraction to repulsion. They may overeat and then starve. These same people, imbalanced, find extremes attractive and this is the source of their disharmony.

Balanced living is neither excess nor deficiency. Neither overeating nor under eating. Never too much, never too little. The result of balanced living is obvious. A balanced person will be at ease. Whatever the situation, their relaxed attitude will not be lost. Unconditionally, the lack of tension will stay. A person who is balanced is always at ease. Even if the death of a loved one comes, and there is grief, they will be at ease: they will receive death as they receive birth. If misery comes they will receive it as they receive joy. Whatever happens it cannot dislodge this person from their place. This relaxed attitude, this ease is a consequence of being balanced.

When the Buddha was dying he asked his followers "why are you weeping? If you would have wept on another day it would have been okay, but this is the last day. Why are you weeping? Do not waste your time in weeping. Treat this day as any other day."

The third key to Personal Harmony is the lack of tension. Lack of tension is one of the great witnesses to the self-actualized person. They are at ease, they do not get stressed under any circumstance and take all of life in their stride. Their mood changes for nothing. Nothing disturbs them; nothing dislocates them from their home in their heart, their centeredness. To such a person you cannot add anything. You cannot take anything away, you cannot add anything, they are fulfilled. Their every breath is a fulfilled breath, silent and blissful they need nothing within. This is the ultimate freedom for everything this person will do they will do out of love, kindness and commitment. There is no hunger, no desperation, and no fear.

Buddha said, "I sit in order to be silent, but sometimes this is too easy, so I walk. But when I walk I carry the same silence within me. I sit, and inside it is the same -- silent. I walk, the inside and outside are the same -- silent" This is the model of a person who has found their True Nature.

We're not talking here about a partial flowering. The great mystics of our time Jesus, Buddha Mohammed, Abraham, they were in their True Nature – totally actualized. If they had dedicated their lives to music then they would have been great musicians too. But their gift was in Spiritual-actualization; they were in love in all circumstances. They were not commercial poets, but their words were poetry, they were not musicians but their message was music of the greatest kind. They were not trying to be specialists but were allowing themselves to simply be their True Nature and allow the beauty of their gifts to flow through their being. You can do this too.

We are not concerned with partial success, or partial growth, we're concerned with total being. You can be centred, you can be grounded, and you can be balanced - always in the middle without effort. As a result you will be at ease at ease with the universe, at home, in relationship and the many things that follow. You will have desire to contribute from within, from your total contentment. You will feel satisfied and comfortable before you leave for work rather than as a result of it. You will not become happier from a win than a loss. A gentleness will descend over your disposition.

The joy of life will be fulfilled for you when you live from your True Nature, because you will understand that you are already fulfilled before you act. Then the world simply becomes a playground in which the differing circumstances of your life come and go. You may decide to change location because you don't like where you are, but this is not in order to make you feel better, inside, you already feel great. Instead it is in order to manifest a different external world out of playful investment, contribution and higher purpose. It is like sitting for dinner with a full stomach. There is no appetite but still sitting at the dinner table is a wonderful way to share time with great friends.

Personal harmony is not only mental it is also physical. You can tell a happy person because their whole energy is centred in their navel area. That means that they understand the balance and centring techniques of the ancient mysteries. The average person lives on the superficial level of life, out of balance and in their head. Their energy is all above their shoulders or way below their navel. You know it when you meet this energy, you can feel it. When you first notice a person the first place you look at them, is where their energy sits.

Happiness can never been known on the surface. We may eat sugar or drink alcohol or dance but unless this happiness is felt deeply then in the morning there is no sense of it. The whole of life in all its beautiful diversity can only be known from this place of our True Nature. Living on the surface then only lukewarm life is possible. It's a great quote that "everybody dies, but not everybody lives." An inauthentic life is a shallow life. It is lived out of balance where high fluctuations of emotional disturbance permeate every event. One drama to the next. It becomes a daily routine of emotional turbulence of high and low, tension and surrender. This is a very unfulfilling existence although on the surface it may look rich and dramatic. It is shallow and in this heart and mind, there is no rest. For this person their interactions become inauthentic because they have not really lived in their true nature. All they have done is danced up and down all day giving the impression of life.

Personal harmony leads to an authentic life, which can become invested in an authentic relationship, and anything that is authentic, is beautiful.

Summary.

- 1. We must separate the inner world from the outer for personal harmony.
- 2. The inner world cannot be satisfied by dogma, philosophy or materiality.
- 3. The outer world seeks things in the pursuit of the inner quest of the soul.
- 4. Nothing of the senses ever satisfied the soul.
- 5. Until beauty can be felt it is not harmonious.
- 6. Beauty exists in all things, events and people.
- 7. Peace of mind, health of the body are the external testaments to personal harmony.
- 8. Disharmony is the breakdown between human thought and natural law. The fight can never be won.

Chapter 2. Harmony in the Mind

In this chapter we present the refinement of our thought process to focus on those thoughts that are productive as the key to creating our own reality. Thoughts of an inharmonious nature create destructive realities (fear, shame, guilt, anger, greed) and thoughts of a harmonious nature create constructive realities (love, care, gratitude, kindness, humility).

Tao de Jing says, "...be as kind as a grandmother; as dignified as a king."

"There are many planes of existence and the material one is on the surface. On this plane we may choose to live out most of our life and so a great journey takes place here. However, there is no security in the world of materials. Human security cannot be achieved through bondage or materiality. Often we become trapped in the transient consciousness of the material realm, hoping that the formality and structure of such a realm can appease hunger for personal harmony we carry within. Security cannot be found like this. The material realm is the smallest drop in the great ocean of life. Absolutely nothing can keep an individual from exploring and discovering that great ocean."

We must come to accept the power that each human being holds in their mind. The power of thought is greater than many of us have imagined. When people are unaware they are blind to the secrets of life. They live a life as a drunk would, dodging obstacles and stepping on things. They do not know what they are doing, either to themselves, or others.

We need to get to know our mind, totally, and honestly. That process begins as we shake free of our ego, to know what's real and what's false. Our ego (identity and beliefs), drives us, motivates us, get's us into and out of trouble; ego is what we defend when we feel judged or criticized. Ego is the platform from which we measure and decide about life. Ego is, for the most part constructed from our experiences, our environmental conditioning or education.

Therefore, this ego is a collection of erroneous facts that, through conditioning, or experience have been adopted as personal truth. But they are far from the real truth; they are just our truth. Our ego is inherited when we are born and gets passed on when we die. It is built on perception rather than fact and, because it drives emotion, is the cause of all human suffering. Consequently, if we don't rise beyond the ego, we do not begin to feel the harmony for which we were born.

Thoughts travel through walls where no feelings pass.

A silent communication exists between people. Every thought that has once crossed the mind, every feeling that passes through one's heart, every word that is once spoken and perhaps never thought of again, and every action once committed and forgotten, is given a place, a life, and it continues to live on afterward. Once given birth to, every thought, word, action or feeling takes on a life of its own. When we express a thought, the action takes only a moment, but the resonance lasts forever.

If a little pebble thrown into the sea and stirs the water, it is hard to comprehend the extent to which this ripple travels. Even a great ocean is influenced by a single stone. We may not be conscious of it, but a single ripple, given the right conditions, has the potential to build into a huge tidal wave. What we can see are only the tiny immediate circles that the pebble produces, but the vibration, which it produced in the sea, reaches much further than we can ever imagine.

Similarly, the universe is like a sea; it is a sea made of the finest fluid. It ripples, flows and transports thought waves to infinite places. Our ears do not hear it and our minds do not know it, but it occurs just the same. Like a radio transmission, signals are sent, of course if no radio is listening, or they are tuned to other frequencies, the signal is not heard, but it exists and impacts the whole of existence.

Our thoughts affect everything and so we have a responsibility not only to those around us, but to ourselves. What we contribute to the creation of this earth is not limited by the material wealth we can offer; it extends to the very thoughts, feelings and the visions that we hold. Therefore, when a person emotionally matures, they begin to feel the deeper responsibilities to the world around them, and it is from this moment that a person truly begins their real life.

Mental disharmony is reflected in the world as greed, anger, violence, jealousy, and deceit, to list a few. While Compassion, love, kindness and generosity have been noted as some of those that come from harmony.

Knowing this, we are invited to become responsible for considering the harmony of every thought we think, and for every feeling that passes through our mind and heart. There is never one moment of our life that is wasted, for life is not just a random existence. If we knew how to direct our thoughts accurately, how to express our words with clarity, how to communicate effectively with our movements, how to live with integrity between thought and action, we could create a perfect, harmonious atmosphere in our life, and those around us.

Harmony is beauty.

Harmony is not only an internal experience it is also recognised externally, through the senses. Harmony is beauty. A thing is deemed beautiful only when its parts are in harmony. The world is called beautiful because everything acts in conformity with nature's laws; it returns to a certain known, it is acting according to its own nature. We call this True Nature for the Earth; the natural rhythm of life and it is the alignment with this True Nature that resonates within us. We find it when we are on track, doing what we love. All beauty is therefore an expression of harmony, and is automatically recognized by our inner being.

In this way we cannot be fooled. There are many people and places which attempt to fake harmony, to decorate the façade of beauty, they look great and smell great, they feel great and act great, but they lack real beauty because they lack harmony. This cannot pass the measure of our instinct because in our true nature there is true knowing. People may be filled with knowledge of life even spiritual realms but if there is no harmony within them, then all that knowledge is useless.

Not only people but also things are affected by harmony or its lack. Thoughts that go into something multiply its effect a thousand fold. The emotional state we are in when we write a letter is worth more than all the words combined. The positive thoughts filling the mind while we cook are more important to our nourishment than the origin and source of the food itself.

The love and care we invest in writing a story, painting a picture or composing a song, is all much more vital than the work itself. Hence, we can expand our thoughts even further to consider how our conscious and subconscious thoughts will affect our own bodies, and potentially that of the people we work with and the person we sleep next to. Continuously plagued with negative thoughts, or living with little gratitude, our bodies will start to reveal the truth of any toxic inner dialogue, leading eventually to physical disease. Most of our disease comes from our mind.

Harmonics of like minds.

There is another interesting aspect in studying personal harmony, and this is that "every mind attracts and reflects thoughts of its own kind". Just as the soil of a certain earthly region may attract flowers of a particular variety to grow while repelling a certain type of weed.

Like is attracted to like. The mind develops a certain character, and the thought pictures of that particular character appeal to like minds. For example, if a thief goes to a city, they will certainly encounter another thief while going about their daily tasks. They recognize each other at once and enjoy similar environments. As soon as their glances meet, a communication will be established, because their thoughts are alike.

There is not one moment when the thought pictures of our character are not present, and so it wields incredible power over people. All of life is a picture in mind form; those pictures in the minds of others that are alike with our pictures are called attractive. This is the basis for most sexual, material and social attraction. A hungry person in need of approval will attract a person of like mind. One will give - the other receives - but the giver is needy and eventually reveals their own appetite. Such is the dynamic of lust.

It is important to distinguish that thoughts do not have to be materialized for a results to occur. They may be purely vibrational in form, but they exist as pictures, dreams, ideas, attitudes, memories long forgotten, consciousness, interests and imaginations. It is said that even before two people meet they know each other's mind on a subconscious level. Then they work to meet on the physical, and experience the reality in the manifestation of those vibrating forms.

It is no different to suggesting that the soul, or its projection, enters the body at birth based on a vibration of consciousness of the parents, and then lives to experience the materialization of that consciousness.

Higher thinking minds, with higher thoughts will always attract minds with higher thoughts. An ordinary mind is attracted toward ordinary thoughts. For instance, a person who has a habit of criticizing people will most often open their ears to the criticism of others, because this is the subject which interests them. Indeed, their level of comfort is found there. A person entrenched in negative thinking cannot resist the temptation of hearing negativity of another person because this is most near to their heart. What is most profound is that they also think like this toward themselves. There is no escaping that what we do unto others, we always do unto ourselves, Therefore, if we are complimentary and compassionate to others, we breed this toward ourselves.

When thoughts are expressed to a person who has no experience of that thought, (they do not exist within the mind of that person), they tend to go ignored or unnoticed. Thoughts that are not already in the heart do not resonate on the same vibration, and therefore fall away. The heart of this individual takes no pleasure in receiving these thoughts, as it will discard anything that is not harmonious. This gives rise to the concept that no one can do to you more than you do to yourself. No one can criticize you more or compliment you more than you. Therefore, the mind world is our kingdom, our property, our future, and our destiny. Whatever we sow, we reap. It begins with mastery over thought.

Chapter 3. Harmony of the Heart

In this chapter we explore the real essence of personal harmony and begin to understand the vast difference between mind and heart as a focus for living.

Your heart is the core of your deepest humanity. When we have finished exploring intellect and attending ceremonies, when we are exhausted trying to change the unchangeable, then we come to rest in our heart. In this place your heart and my heart are one, we are interconnected, no need to compare, we are a part of something bigger, where our individuality is transient, the moment becomes important and we all relax in the knowledge that we have no idea of what could happen next. This is a beautiful reality, the core of confidence, love, beauty and a healthy life.

If one spent their whole life doing nothing other than opening their heart and developing the qualities of the heart, it is no exaggeration to say that this effort alone would bring them to the highest goal of human life. Because it is through the heart that one finds their truth and within the heart that one finds their True Nature. In this place –Self and God are one. You have to know this totally. To separate God and Self is to think God is great and I am small. Then you are locked in to your own smallness, and you cannot see the connection between what is natural, beautiful, and you. Native people knew this connection before religion came and separated them from nature. It is the human heart that can teach us to love without condition. It is here that strength and conviction emanate. Compassion and loving-kindness live in the heart and it is here that one feels peace. It is through the heart that we can find the way to treat our brothers and sisters, and ultimately, a way to be true to ourselves.

The heart represents the essential nature of a person and thus the development of the heart; the unfolding of the heart and the illumination of the heart are of the utmost importance on the path of to find your True Nature. This is the centre around which your life can revolve. But it is not the emotional centre. The heart is often mistaken as a nice fuzzy feeling in the centre of the chest. This is the emotional centre. We are talking about the human spirit. It is not a feeling but rather a knowing. Called the inner voice, it is not a voice at all. Called the spirit it is not a physical existence. It is a pure, unconditional knowing. No words can describe it.

To find your heart is to find your path, a path that doesn't waver, it's also to hold a certain centre, and be true to yourself and others. It all begins with gaining a true sense of your being. It's a way to think and feel that reflects your true nature, it is natural, and, it creates a certain inner confidence, a strength, and builds a foundation from which your life may evolve. It can't be separate practice from daily life because it is life itself. It doesn't mean rushing around solving the world's problems either, because those obstacles are countless and that rushing around is in itself part of the world's problems. By listening to your own heart, to your own particular gifts, it enables you to focus on what you really love to do and to express yourself without tension or reaction. The deepest experience of life is awakened when each individual finally takes this opportunity. We become the mirror of the change we would love to see in the world; we must first learn to love ourselves and to find peace and harmony within.

When we explore the term heart in common language we find that 'heart' means the central or innermost part of something such as the 'heart of the city', it also means the essential or vital part of something such as "what is the heart of the matter?" A person with a 'lot of heart' is someone with determination. To 'lose heart' means to be discouraged so we see that the will of a person emanates from their heart. We refer to the heart when we talk about generosity or sincerity as well as consideration, understanding and helpfulness as when we say, "He has a big heart." or "She is a dear heart." When a person is cruel or mean or when someone shows no regard for others we say, "His heart is closed or small or cold or that he has no heart at all."

In most of the spiritual traditions of the world the heart is considered the location where heaven and earth meet within the human being. This, of course, is not the physical heart but rather the 'heart centre' within the chest. This centre is where we experience love; it's the Temple within.

As humans cannot grasp the idea of a heart outside the body, there is a part in this body of flesh dedicated to housing the idea of the heart. This area is most sensitive to feeling and has been called "broken" at times, although no physical break actually occurs.

The surface of our being is mind, while the depth of it is heart. The heart is clarity the mind is personality. It is through the heart that we feel ourselves or know ourselves. Once a person understands their True Nature, the character and the mystery of heart, they understand the language of the whole of creation because they know truth. So we have choices. Listen to this heart or listen to the mind and its stories or fear and uncertainty.

It takes a certain trust A trust that, when faced with what seems to be an insurmountable challenge, we will survive. It does not necessitate becoming religious. The spiritual life is not lived in temples, or on particular days of worship, nor is it only reverence to a statue or icon; it is lived every single moment of our lives. From what people see of us, and what we think, to our secret thoughts and our secret ideas.

People say put your heart into it; it means to become fully invested. It means to throw the full weight of your humanity behind something. There are no half hearted success stories. We must be vigilant. Our heart must remain invested. When the heart goes out of something we automatically sabotage it. So, if we can invest ourselves in maintaining the commitment of our heart we will automatically achieve many of our dreams in life.

Chapter 4. Harmony and Personality

In this chapter we explore the process of sustaining personal harmony and how to bring it to the real world of everyday life.

"Reality replied: O prisoner of time,
I was a secret treasure of kindness and generosity,
And I wished this treasure to be known,
So I created a mirror: its shining face, the heart;
Its darkened back, the world;
The back would please you if you've never seen the face."

Rumi

Friendly attitude.

A friendly attitude, expressed in sympathetic thought, speech, and deed, is the principal experience of personal harmony. There is limitless scope to show this attitude, and however much this personality is developed in this way, it is never too much. The tendency to give is what shows great dignity. One can never do too much. To do more than one's due is perhaps the ideal, giving more than taking, this will accomplish one's life purpose.

Sincerity.

As a gift is nothing without the giver, so care is nothing without a harmonious personality, it alone gives value to the receiver. Therefore a note written without true feelings of the writer has no effect; the harmony of the person who writes will shine in between the lines of text. Their spirit, their love, their kindness, will all help to make the gift, the song, the poem or the product and service, valuable and effective. We must really be mindful to hold this care because it is sincerity.

Graciousness.

As soon harmony is felt within it comes alive in the form of graciousness. Monks and priests are trained in the art of graciousness, yet it is born in the heart of mankind naturally.

Graciousness is quite different from the mask, which is labelled patronizing. Gracious people are truly humble. The great ones, the truly noble people, are gracious because they are more sensitive to all the hurt and harm that exists in life. They do not hide from an awareness of the actions of those who are unripe. Their eyes are open and from this there is a compulsion to help. Out of this come kindness and a desire for betterment for others.

The value of humility, which is expressed in graciousness, will always be valued. It is easy to know the idea, but most difficult to practice graciousness through life, because there is no end to the opportunities to live it's opposite. It is a significant diligence that is required to master every thought that precedes every action in life. We need a habit of good judgment and a fair sense of integrity measuring all one does. It needs a fine sense of art and beauty, for in refining the personality, and entering mindfulness about life, one chooses to hold the highest thoughts, and continually witness the beauty, which is always naturally occurring, in every moment. Consider the cultivation of this ability to see beauty in all things, at all times, one of the most humane attributes of life. Find this and you will know the essence in which lies the fulfilment of the dreams and missions of life, this can become ones religion.

It begins in Nature.

Act with care.

Gandhi used to say. "Before you act, consider the affect of that act on the poorest person you ever met in your life, and ask whether the thing I'm about to do will benefit them, and if it doesn't, don't do it." This is pure intention. This is Gandhi's way of checking in on himself, "am I acting from truth?"

John's heart was cold. His wife had left him for another man. His anger for this other man grew daily. He thought about this other man every time he ate, every time he watched television, when he jogged on the beach or did his sit-ups, he thought how much he would love to brutally attack and maim this other man. Day by day by day he injected into himself thoughts of vindication and reprisal. The bitterness ate into his bones, into his teeth and changed their colour, his eyes changed, his ears changed their volume, until finally he was invaded by his own bitterness and he became the result of his own thoughts; toxic.

We must learn to act with care, and be mindful to put goodness behind our action as a motive. This is a great key to youthfulness and great health.

Self Reliance.

Self-reliance is an essential ingredient if you are to live in harmony. You must know yourself. This is not the ego, or emotional, or feeling – it is beyond these transitory experiences of life. Learning to think for yourself, to look after yourself, to wait on yourself, and to act on your own judgments is a crucial part of the development of the freedom of spirit. To get past convention as a measure of your worth is essential.

All humans are dependent, socially, commercially, nationally, and emotionally. Therefore self-reliance is not isolation or withdrawal but the ability to follow your own convictions amongst the questions and turbulence of life. You must become immune. A conviction must arise in you where there is no need to go into defence, no mention of doubt or uncertainty, no panic or fear, just centred, committed and certain.

Base your actions upon your own consciousness. Know that you cannot be right without wrong. Move beyond reacting, trickery and manipulation. Be real, honest with yourself and others. You are free to be and there is no need to pretend. Get past malice, emotion and anger. Get past retribution and condemnation because these are all signs of stupidity, ignorance and unconsciousness and truly – if your mission becomes to reach for your deeper truth, those are the blockages. If you are poor and ignorant, or deficient in any important range of education use your time for study and pursue a line of study that will better your circumstances. If you are poor uneducated and in fair health it's your fault that you remain poor. Financial independence is within the power of every human being who is not in poor health. Self-effort is the first law of success. Poverty is usually the result of a lack of discipline and self-effort.

Arrange your life so that mental health does not become a hindrance. Adhere to the laws of balance in all your mental activity. See that be getting elated will breed a depression. Acknowledge that righteousness, the idea that you are right, is the cause of all mental diseases. Breakthrough your expectations. Expectations are the root of all breakdowns. Expectations are like the contamination that breeds suffering. If you can be a person whose expectations become the most flexible part of their world then you will develop the heart of a monk, a rabbi or a priest of the highest order in everyday life.

Use the fuel of emotions to build your life rather than to destroy it. Emotions are natural and wonderful but to follow them, to use emotions, as a guide in your life is the poorest of all religions. Emotions are there to awaken you, to enlighten you, to absorb you in life but they are not the outcome of your life. Emotions connect you to life and earth, but they are the joker, they mislead you, they provoke you and ultimately you must, in the interests of life mastery and the spirit of your dreams see them for their fallacy. Emotions are not life, but your reaction to it.

Dissolve tension – Living openly.

If you turn your attention inside of yourself every day if you will open your mind and heart to feel the flow of energy within yourself you begin to feel your awareness of it expand – then the issues in your life become, smaller and finally, no issues at all. Your notion of who is living your life and who is motivating your body totally changes. Furthermore your understanding and experience of the creative power of life in its fullest sense brings you to a total acceptance of your life within a larger scheme of life itself. You begin to embrace a real appreciation for the opportunities you have to interact and communicate with this gift of life, in any form. Then, whatever dance you do, whatever game you play, it becomes merely the arena in which you discover and express your interchange with this creative flow. Whenever we feel energy spinning in our head, it means that we're not doing something right, and at that moment we need to take a breath, relax for a moment, and feel what the energy in our head is about.

You must learn to open without getting lost. You have to remember who you are and where you are going, putting this in the context of the inner effort you make to remain open.

This is necessary so that the energies you absorb and consume, and the expansion that results, will re articulate in your life in concrete, practical and beneficial ways which will serve you and all the people whose lives are connected to you. Only in this way will you really learn about energy –about the subtle energy of life itself.

Gentleness.

Gentleness is the principal thing that evolves from an experience of personal harmony; one can see how gentleness works as the principal thing in every art. Anger, frustration, stress and violence then, are the enemy of the dance. Gentleness should be the aim. Do no harm becomes the motto of true harmony. And this is the true nature of most of humanity. When we care for each other we feel an innate sense of truth and wholeness.

Vanity is separateness, and this is the defence of the weak. Truly honest individuals will recognize themselves in the heart of another and, rather than judge them as less, will have empathy. It is of no service to humanity to judge another as less. It is of service to acknowledge our own humility. So much of life's stresses can be extinguished at the source if we are able to recognize ourselves in others.

Dignity.

Dignity, which in other words may be called self-respect, is also at the heart of this inner harmony. When one asks, "what it is, and how this principle can be practiced?" the answer is:

"True dignity is raw honesty"

So for a wise person, reality provides the beauty in which true nature is recognized. It is seen in light and dark and this gives balance to their personality. Wisdom gives that weight; seeking the balance is the mark of wisdom. Foolishness at its core is worry, anxiety, stress, and giving ones power to others through concern over that which cannot be changed. To emote on matters of opinion or reaction is unproductive. Wisdom alone brings freedom and when we free another to be themselves we free ourselves.

The more one studies and understands what exists at the heart of humanity, the more one finds that it is the integrity of dignity that creates the forward movement and purpose of our lives. All the different virtues, nobility, integrity, compassion, and inner beauty, are the outcome of an integrity to the true nature of things.

If you can try to be in the moment, quiet and not talk too much, you will know a deeper awareness of life. Fast response to challenge is not likely to result in anything thoughtful, so the best thing to do is to be as quiet as possible, and to think about matters for a while before reacting. Even if somebody says I want to know right away. You can say, Well, I don't know right this second, but I'll tell you tomorrow. You should avoid answering in the moment of a reaction. This is dignity of the highest order, silence.

Inner calm

The paths to this inner calm are many, and it seems, everyone thinks their clock alone tells the correct time. Christians claim to possess exclusive truth. Countless varieties of Hindus insist that their sect, no matter how small and insignificant, expresses the ultimate position. Devout Muslims maintain that the Koran supersedes all others. The entire world is being driven insane by this single phrase; "my religion alone is true". The greatest gift belongs to no one. Ideals cannot be entirely accurate. When we have stilled the waters of the mind, created outcomes that are filled with integrity and provided an experience of life that is harmonious with both self and other, then we have truly found a true path. It is an experience and we should experiment until we actually find and sustain it. Beyond theory and ideology, we must seek to experience this in ourselves first.

To cultivate this inner truth one must occasionally come forth from the conventional environment into the spaciousness of exploration and test new ways. One must also retire now and then into seclusion, to sit peacefully in the clear waters of solitude. Then we can return to the denser, more obscure realms of social responsibility, without becoming disorientated by them.

If the mind is still then, the body will be happy. One must find out how to become happy within by achieving this inner calm. Wanting to reform the world without discovering one's true self is like trying to cover the whole world with leather to avoid pain of walking on stones and thorns, it is of course, much simpler to wear shoes.

Daily ritual – Inner work.

Many people go out into life, and then they meet with all the contracted energies and every other complexity that could obstruct their efforts. And then, only after all that, do they to think about their spiritual practice as something to tack on when all the "important" things have been taken care of. Not surprisingly, by that point a person feels "Oh, I'm too tired already" and gives up on the idea of developing a spiritual practice.

Start each day with your inner work, and as you move through the day, you will meet each opportunity that presents itself from your own centre, and then you establish a sense of joy, vitality and enthusiasm for life. You engage this joy, you dance with it: Then whatever the activity, it is not even work any more – it's an act of love. You find that you're tireless in it; you have all the energy you require for anything. It is a question of where you begin, and of what you understand your real work to be. Try to start out with an intense love of life, and an intense love of your creator. Then go where ever that love takes you and do whatever you are called upon to do from there.

Pain and suffering.

"Fear and Pain never disappear. Divine has two aspects –pain and bliss – they never disappear they are always present and are close together. Subtle balance. Pain and joy are one in the same experience."

Nothing is without pain, yet there is a big difference between pain and suffering. Pain is when you cut your hand. You don't worry because you know it will get better. Suffering is when you're not sure and you worry about what is going to happen. If you live from tension or from need, from drama or from difficulty, then what you get back will be tension, need, drama, and suffering. If you live from lightness, joy and love then what you get back will be pleasure and pain, it is very different; yet, endlessly the same.

To see beyond the chemistry of your body – through the cloud, is the challenge. To do this you must cultivate the capacity to deal with pain. The only way to do this is to open your heart to it every day, to surrender to it.

Let it come inside without resisting it in the slightest, let it penetrate you as deeply as it wants, and then to work its way through you. This requires a real effort. It requires that you learn to allow all of the tensions and all of the energy and power of life itself to reach deeply into you and change you automatically.

Seek balance.

In all of this, the fundamentally important aspect is the feeling with which you live your life, and from which you express your concern. When I say to be aware of what is inside, I do not mean being aware of feeling jealous or happy or sad. All of that is nonsense, and most people simply use such circumstances in life to become hysterical or dramatic. Instead, I mean having a sense of vitality for life and of the simple joy within you, no matter what goes on around you. Knowing that everywhere you look there are two sides, that beauty exists in all things to the conscious person who thinks on a higher plane and that harmony, inner harmony is simply a matter of resignation to the beauty of what is.

Don't react – Reaction causes disharmony.

"Start with some composure – some self-control and heightened sense of awareness to increased concentration on the moment."

During challenge it is important not to react. Try to be in the moment, quietly, and do not talk too much. Fast response to challenge is not likely to result in anything thoughtful. The best thing is to be as quiet as possible, and to think about the matter for while before expressing your reaction.

In any case, the real challenges are not always random and spontaneous. The real challenges are the ones that keep coming up over and over again. They challenge our limited understanding, our limited capacity, and the ways in which our emotions and our minds inhibit the flow of our creative energy. Small things add up and make us easily distracted.

Remember, you always have choice as to how you respond to any situation. There is a wise way and a not wise way. Wise is to see the balance, the two sides of it and then choose the action, unwise is to see one side of a thing and then react, one is powerful and truth, the other is illusion, it is a choice.

"There is only one way to be bound to anyone. And that is by love. Being bound by love is not being bound at all. It's liberation."

Focus on what you have.

"When you stop praying for what you think is missing, and simply attune yourself to the extraordinary richness, the quality and the love that are at the core if your heart the ocean itself becomes apparent, and all the rest is just the debris that floats on the surface. All debris, it is dead; the ocean is what is alive."

The door of my heart is open

The door of my heart is open
To you, and you and you
It is open to the sky and to the earth
To the pain and to each new birth
The door of my heart is open
The door of my heart is open to the terrorist
You cannot consume my life
The door of my heart is open to the religions
All seeking the holy path
And the door of my heart is open to you
My friend, my enemy or my wife
The door of my heart cannot be closed
By ideas, ideals or myth
The door of my heart is awakened to all
Nature is harmony, beauty and love
The door to my heart complete
The door of my heart consumes your violence
And embraces the depth of your soul
The door of my heart awakens to live
And gives away grasping to control

Self respect.

Bringing personal harmony into our lives is like growing up. Respect and dignity, ethics and integrity are birthed in this way. It is not always this easy. A childlike approval by others, sometimes never leaves and so a personal morality is never birthed. Then, they may feel that their opinion of themselves is less important than what others think.

Moving from external approval to internal is vital to personal harmony. If this integrity exists within us, then the action is automatically increased in its merit. Mistakes may happen but from the heart there can be no ill intent. The outer world becomes a stage and the inner world a garden. Under this situation tension and self-sabotage will evaporate. When you have a good relationship with yourself, you will have a morality within you that is "uncompromisable."

Psychotic behaviour is when the inner world has no conscience – no sense of right or good. Under these circumstances when what others think about us, is more important than what we think, we are birthed into a world of self-loathing. Masks become our investment.

Beyond fear.

We try to live too long. Harmony does not come from life extension: life extension comes from harmony. It is essential to deal with fears and come to enjoy each day as if it were our last. "Everybody dies, but not everybody lives."

Patience.

It seems that, in order to learn that noble manner of life, what is most needed is patience - sometimes in the form of endurance, sometimes in the form of consideration, and sometimes in the form of forgiveness. But, most of all it requires the ability to overcome frustration. To see that we are powerless in some circumstances. It is wisdom to know the true limit of ones capacity to influence another. Changing others is not a high ambition. Sometimes the greatest nobility is allowing others to live their path.

It is too often that we see people loose dignity in the attachment to another's journey. In particular in family where children and parents are at war in a very unnatural way. How is this possible? A family is meant to hold together, but there is personality here too, ego, often most difficult personality because there is no patience. There is the most confronting experience to be unable to change another in family because these are the ones we love most. We wish to become most strong in family in order to create happiness in those we love. And in becoming strong one becomes blind and impatient. To maintain humility is the beginning of true harmony. Humility is the confession of openness; that the most powerful way to change somebody, and breed their happiness is not to want them to change at all.

Avoid righteousness.

Any efforts made in developing the personality or in character-building must not be made for the sake of proving oneself superior to others, but in order to become more agreeable to those around us and to those with whom we comes in contact. Conciliation is a high ideal of the heart. Conciliation is removal of judgment. Truly one can develop the habit - desire the best for others. Not invented compassion, nor exclusive to any race or religion, is a true ownership that all people, are equal, and ultimately therefore all people, no matter what their behaviour, are a reflection of ourselves.

When we begin to impose ideals on others, there is a contamination of the beauty of the heart. Our judgment of what is right for others is shallow and contaminated with our own personality. What one thinks is best for another, is complete loss if humility, a righteousness of mind. There is no heart in the righteous mind, and so, once we are seeking to make it better for others in any way by changing them to our way of living there is automatically a dislodgement of our own integrity. "Do unto others as you would have them do unto you" and the best is, leave them alone, and love them for who they are.

This is most apparent in times of distress. In this age, advice is cheap. We all seem to think we have the solution to everyone else's problems. But it is more accurate to say that we have "a" solution and that solution is not right but might be right. And often even this is illusion. It is truly interesting to see teachers in this new age sharing wisdom, which, if one were to examine the life of the teacher, doesn't work. I know so many teachers of spirituality who have a terribly traumatic relationship. I know business coaches who have never done anything except be an employee. What good is their teaching if it did not manifest in their own life. Righteousness is killing us. It is causing – as it always has, wars and abuse. Avoid it at all cost.

Personal harmony means that a person remains balanced. Their life is balance. They are never one-sided, they never make a stand, they are never righteous because they understand that everything in this world is built in duality and therefore to stand on one side or the other breeds imbalance. That imbalance is the ego and lives – feeds off -emotion. Emotion is a habit; so finding balance in everything breaks most addictions and illness.

"Seek the balance in all things and you will become of the Master. You will witness ever-deeper appreciation for beauty in nature. You will witness the magnificence in this universe and you will hold in your heart the appreciation for yourself as a reflection of that creation."

Christopher Walker

Personal harmony means that you see every event in a balanced way. This is mastery, to see all events as both good and bad, attractive and unattractive, supportive and challenging, masculine and feminine, healthy and unhealthy. The unharmonious mind will bring the past into the present as good or bad, right or wrong, attractive or unattractive. The emotions will seek the greatest imbalance in order to create drama. Drama is important to those people who seek approval because drama is the source of other people's opinion of us. The more the righteous mind can see an event in an imbalanced away the more it is satisfied and comfortable with its knowing. But this knowing is pure delusion. If you were to buy a car and think that there is only good news to be gained from this purchase you will soon learn the delusion of this is experience. But the deluded person goes on seeking one-sided events in order to satisfy the ego, mind, security, and their mind is always disturbed because they are continually surprised.

Think love.

When you are in love you become love. When you are in love you become the embrace. You forget yourself so totally that you can say, "I am no more - only love exists" then the heart is not beating but love is beating, and the blood is not circulating, love is circulating. The eyes are not seeing, love is seen. Then hands are not moving to touch, love is moving to touch.

Without love, life becomes dry. Sex without love is a sport. Sport without love is a chore. Chores without love cause anguish and stress. And stress without love causes death. In fact, love is always here in the moment. To the wise person every single event can be seen as love. The wisest is the one who sees the order in the chaos fastest. But to see order in the chaos you have to know the laws of nature. Like "no one gets beaten up more than they do to themselves". And there are no victims, and "what you judge you breed."

It's all love and that's the ultimate beauty. Harmony comes from beauty so the ultimate thought is one of love. Love is beauty and beauty is love. And what is beauty? Ancient Greek teachings say "beauty is symmetry, proportion and order" things in a certain sacred proportion. Universal definitions are a bit broader, but no different: support and challenge is the beauty of love, balance. That's how we are always loved. We are always supported and challenged.

Eliminate tension.

When we live off balance we create tension. And that is a constant turmoil: anguish. If you are not on centre you are not where you should be; you're not at you're right balance. Being off-balance is the basis of all mental tension. Tension is unconsciousness. It is a very poor basis for decisions and action, never act from tension because it creates desperation. If it becomes too much, you go mad. A mad person is one who has gone out of themselves completely. They are so out of balance they have fallen off the edge. Mental health problems come to the "all or nothing people." Black and white fundamentalism in any walk of life, that's the madness. Those people run around saying, "I've got to do this and I have to have that". That's madness in the making. When the mind is so split into right and wrong, the heart cannot exist.

The enlightened person is the complete opposite – they see two sides in everything, and therefore the universal beauty exists for them, in everything.

Be flexible.

Disharmony can be felt when we experience anger. Actually, this is madness, but it's hopefully not permanent. The quality of the anger is identical to that of the mad person, but it doesn't last as long. The other extreme is experienced when we touch our centre and in this moment we are no different to the great masters who've walked this earth. We are a Buddha, a Christ or a Krishna, the only difference is ours is only temporary, theirs is/was permanent. Really the moment you have recognized that you have moved to the centre you will think, "wow look at me – I feel amazing" and therefore get off centre in that thought.

Live life totally – be real.

Most people have learned to temper their lives in such a way that they experience only small degrees of anything. They have learned to control their madness, emotion, and therefore they never really experience life fully. If you are always cutting short the experience of emotions you do not know yourself either. So most people are living dead, caught between the two extremes of full experience of life and the absolute centre of their True Nature. You will notice many artists, great artists, painters and poets, they are not 'normal'. They are liquid. They touch the centre sometimes and sometimes they go out to the limits. They move very fast between these two points. The anguish can be extreme, the tension is high, they live between two worlds, constantly changing themselves. And that's why they feel it is important that they have no identity. They feel that they are outsiders. In the world of normality they are outsiders because they really experience the two extremes. It is a total life experience from the centre of their heart – inspired; to the extreme of emotion life has to offer.

There are four different types of people related to the different experiences of centring. The first has a fixed identity. They feel solid and they say they know who they are. Their identity is fixed to the career they choose. They say, "I am a doctor, a lawyer, a train driver a professor." These people constantly cling to their identity, to the image portrayed by what they do. This is a fearful life because if the job goes wrong, they do too. They are the obsessive-compulsive types.

The next are those who live liquid images -- poets, artists, painters, and singers. They do not know who they are at all. Sometimes they go to one extreme and are inspired and at other times they go mad with emotion, sometimes they touch the ecstasy and sometimes they touch the drama, madness. So they often use substances to regulate or even stimulate the switch. If they are extreme they use substance to centre and visa versa. So these people often don't know how to just be calm. Their heart is always searching and getting exhausted, a random life with occasional passages of brilliance and contentment.

The third group are those who are permanently mad. They have gone outside themselves; they never come back into their home, their heart. They do not even remember that they have a home. Or where they left the keys. They are in the wilderness because emotion took over. They loose concentration before they get it. They talk and smoke and constantly fidget. They forget things, they forget a lot. These people are beyond the confines of the mind and often need pharmaceuticals to stabilize them. Even if the mind does come stable they may sabotage their life, work, relationship, wealth or happiness because they just can't stand their own company. Emotion is the perfect antidote to self-disgust. Drama is the companion of the person who does not like their mind.

And forth of those who have reached their home, Buddha, Christ, Krishna, and stayed there. They have reached their home; it is a totally relaxed environment. They are fully conscious there is no tension, no effort, and no desire. In one word, there is nothing to become, no want, contentment. They do not want to become anything. They are, and they have been. No becoming. And they are at ease with their being. They don't want to change anything. Whatsoever they are, they are at ease with it. They do not want to change it, do not want to go anywhere. They are not worried about the future. That does not mean the Buddha will not eat or a Buddha would not sleep. But a Buddha will not project their desires; they will not eat tomorrow, they will eat today. This person has found their True Nature and can bring this into everyday life in a powerful way.

Embrace the chaos of your life – it is growth.

Maximum evolution occurs at the border of chaos and order. We have an opportunity to see our lives with this universal perspective. Rather than define the chaos and calamity of our life as failures, we can more wisely say chaos, the essential nature of growth. Rather than illness it is chaos, rather than divorce or heartbreak we can see chaos, which is natural. Chaos is the flip side of order. Just as love has the balance of support and challenge, the other side of order is chaos. So the chaos in our life is the other half of the peace of our life. Through chaos we are driven to grow, evolve. Rather than shrink from the opportunity to grow we can welcome chaos, welcome the opportunity to find balance, to be thankful. So, a universal perspective of life is not pitiful, although this is an honest expression, the universal perspective always sees the opportunity to grow, and growth can only be measured in perspective.

Not competitive.

A person who is in harmony never makes a stand. They do not build a sense of identity out of being unique. When, as the great mystics were able to do, we can say I am no better or worse than anybody else we free ourselves. It's beyond judgment of right and wrong, beyond individuality as a measure of a person's worth. Then the perfect golf swing comes, the perfect tennis shot, the perfect football rush comes. Not when you are trying to beat someone, that's identity and ego. It comes when there's no tension. You are free to follow the path. This is the flow, the zone of life. There is no other thing like it.

You don't win Olympic gold trying to beat people, you win Olympic gold when you stop trying to do your personal best, and just do it. REMEMBER competition is the lowest level of consciousness and therefore, the lowest level of your sustainable performance.

See yourself in others – Individuality is a myth.

With children – you don't bring them up best by comparing who they are to some arbitrary standard you got. You free them by respect and love and by seeing their gifts. People become as we treat them. They, like you, are a perfect balance of good news and bad, and the wise parent knows it, but focuses on the good news (called strengths by some).

People do not thrive by putting them in boxes that have negative labels like ADD or depression. When we see our family it is wiser to say, " There is no separation between me and my child. What I see in them is in me in a different form. Therefore if there's nothing I need to change in them, it is all worthy of love in them, as it is in me. But if we don't like ourselves, we can easily start trying to change that aspect of us by eliminating it in them.

If they are hyperactive it's because you can't concentrate on one thing at a time. If they are ADD then you lack discipline. It's always a mirror.

Individuality is the awareness of separation, which we call, ME. That is: individuality is that idea of separate thought, separate emotion, "I am I and I have a right to be an individual." As an individual a person has become conscious of their separate action. This desire for a separate identity forces people to enter into work they hate, activities they don't understand, vocations that are boring attempting to prove something, to create a sense of individuality. Individuality is not harmonious; it is a fiction.

Rather than seeking "identification with individuality" you might find more harmony in your heart if you say, "I am no better or worse than anybody else. I am clever as well as dumb, I am happy and sometimes sad, I am right and equally wrong, I am nice and sometimes mean, I am humble and, at the same time proud, I am success and I am a failure." Then you can stop trying to be different and wasting all that time on identity and get on with life and loving people for who they are, just like you. Once this is accomplished you are beginning to develop some sense of personal harmony.

Diversity is harmony.

The greater appreciation you have for diversity, the greater can be your harmony. The more you can be real the more power and harmony you can have. It's like watching the movie, you are sitting in your seat, there are emotions and feelings on the screen and yet, you are still on your seat. You have a home in your heart, from which you can understand the emotions and dynamics of the world, but it is a movie, the reality is harmonious within you.

The key to this is not to get caught trying to be one side without the other, seeing both sides – finding the balance. Sadness and happiness at the same time. And then not react to either. One man in a consult argued strongly, this is impossible. He quoted his favourite example, "Disneyland" he said with a smirk, "I went to Disneyland and I had an absolute 100% positive experience. All upside."

I questioned him, "Hmmm you defied the laws of the universe did you?"

He replied, "yup, your laws are your laws, not mine."

But lucky for us, his wife was in the room. I appealed to her for a more objective analysis.

She was firm, "Darling, come on, you know the downside" – She helped him start, "what about the long queues that frustrated you, and the cost we spent a year paying the credit card, and the 5 kg of weight you put on, and the sunburn you got, and what about the bunion on your toe, and the depression you got when you got back. And what about the heart murmurs the doctor blamed on your overdoing it, and what about the lost passport in the hotel and our daughter getting lost. What about the fight we had in the queue while waiting for hours and hours so you could have another ride on the train." I stopped her.

He looked sheepishly at me, "well there were some downsides."

I responded, "I know. It's universal law."

STAY CLOSE, MY HEART

Stay close, my heart, to the one who knows your ways;
Come into the shade of the tree that always has fresh flowers.
Don't stroll idly through the bazaar of the perfume-markers:
Stay in the shop of the sugar-seller.
If you don't find true balance, anyone can deceive you;
Anyone can trick out of a thing of straw,
And make you take it for gold
Don't squat with a bowl before every boiling pot;
In each pot on the fire you find very different things.
Not all sugarcanes have sugar, not all abysses a peak;
Not all eyes possess vision, not every sea is full of pearls.
O nightingale, with your voice of dark honey! Go on lamenting!
Only your drunken ecstasy can pierce the rock's hard heart!
Surrender yourself, and if you cannot be welcomed by the friend,
Know that you are rebelling inwardly like a thread
That doesn't want to go through the needle's eye!
The awakened heart is a lamp; protect it by the hem of your robe!
Hurry and get out of this wind, for the weather is bad.
And when you've left this storm, you will come to a fountain;
You'll find a Friend there who will always nourish your soul.
And with your soul always green, you'll grow into a tall tree
Flowering always with sweet light-fruit, whose growth is interior.

Rumi

Raw honesty - own the feeling.

People try to stay true to themselves by blocking out those things they don't like. They become tight and aloof. But life cannot be lived in honesty by blocking it out. It's not by blocking the stream, or damming the river, of feeling that we stay centred, but by opening the sleuth gates and allowing it all to enter, do its work and pass without reaction. Ordinarily people are not the witness but are more likely to be identified with their thoughts. They are attached. They can't separate their feelings from who they are. They feel something and say, "I feel this and I feel that." And in saying so they can't even separate their feelings from who they are so they can't remain in contentment even the tiniest mishap makes them angry or tearful. This is the ego at work. They are in the Matrix and they don't even know it. And eventually the doctor will prescribe a new drug to enable the ignorance to continue.

For example: If anger is there, people become angry, they are united as one with thought, feeling and expression. Identified with thought they move with thought. They become the thought and so they are swinging in drama and emotion all their life, following transient ideals, getting into relationships and jobs that are not wise. They take the form of the thought. But anger is the fire in the belly and any man who does not learn to feel his anger and define it as chi or life force cannot manage it. He becomes it, and explodes like a bomb when the least appropriate time is available for it. You have to become the witness, and then you can see thoughts or feelings running like clouds in the sky. It is raw honesty. You see the depth of your humanity, your reactions and feelings, you feel them, but they are not you. You are actually watching them, even laughing at the anger, holding it rather than drumming it out, celebrating the power of it and then making a choice to express that life force not by emotional release but through focusing it into your love, passion and vision in life.

Become the witness.

Always remember to observe whether harmony is involved in your activities. If it is not involved, then you are probably feeling off balance, in which case it's better not to do anything. Just don't do it. Preserve the energy for the moment when something real happens to you; then do it. Don't smile a false smile; preserve the energy.

When you are in harmony the smile will be natural and real, it will come from your heart and it will change completely, it will be total and every cell of our body will smile. This is the best time to act and make choices in your life.

Rise beyond grief.

Grief need only take a few hours if we are at our True Nature, feeling the harmony. But if we can't see the perspective, if we are attached then we are going to grieve for years. And in these days, that is a very difficult drain on our productive life, and creative expression. That's why personal harmony is so vital. One mother I met had been in grief for months and months after her mother had died, and although her mother was over 80 and had been ill for quite some time, the lady felt obligated to stay in grief for a long time. Meanwhile her own children were totally abandoned, and in those months there was irreparable harm done.

Deal with negative feelings.

To sustain equilibrium in personal harmony is to learn to accept whatever you are. This is the basic footnote, total acceptance. And only through total acceptance can you grow. Through this you can then use all the energy you have. Accept your pain instead of pushing it away. You cannot change the fact that you are human and you have experiences. We must learn to let those feelings; experiences in and then let them out in the same breath. Those energies are a part of the great mystery of life. You must accept that you are everything and therefore it's OK – healthy to feel things positive and negative. We must, however, not hold them for more than a breath. If you can except this and dance with every energy your life will be harmonious and growth will occur naturally.

Loose the blind ambition – Be thankful for what you have.

When we shake off the heaviness of that blind drive for achievement, the ego, we feel joyous; we feel light and with this comes the inner harmony we all so naturally want. This shaking off is more a natural release, a quiet confidence in the result, a non-reactive process. All the qualities we desire, such as gentleness, tolerance, forgiveness, love and appreciation come by being light in mind, soul and body. This is the result of staying connected to your True Nature, personal harmony.

Every action, every word, every feeling you have, and every sentiment you express need to be harmonious. There must be caring, gentleness and conviction. It is not by following someone else's beliefs, or making one's life a religion that is necessary. It is by being a religion, becoming conscious, and expressing a personality that is in tune with Nature that will create harmony within and without. It must be, first and foremost, authentic.

Gratitude is a vital key. Harmony comes from the natural life, which is formed from a thankful heart. You cannot be unhappy and thankful at the same time. When that thankfulness life comes forth, it lightens all the burdens that humans have. Heart and mind aligned are joyous. It makes life smooth. But when there is no appreciation, no receptivity, we sink like a rock to the bottom of the sea. We must learn to float through gratitude.

Gratefulness in the character is like fragrance in the flower, it builds the sincerity that brings integration. A person, however well aligned and qualified in their life's work, who lacks gratefulness, is missing that beauty in their character, which makes the personality alive, attractive and vital. If we answer every little deed with appreciation, we develop in our nature, the spirit of gratefulness; if we have the courage to answer every deed of disturbance with gratefulness we are absolutely exhibiting our True Nature; and by learning this we rise to that state where we begin to realize and share harmony with others. We can never be grateful enough – it is our way of demonstrating truly inspired compassion.

Stay humble.

Humility is one of the greatest keys to Personal Harmony. It should become the greatest of human aspirations. Humility means the music of the soul. It means a healthy dynamic between people, a freedom of expression, the appreciation of beauty, art and music and it is the solace of inner tranquillity, sustainable though all of the worst circumstances.

Immortal people have left behind clues to their secrets of how to live on earth with the great knowledge that they were entrusted with. They were ordinary mortal people from any walk of life, who were humble to their extraordinary and immortal awareness.

They had to be humble. Obedience was the key. They all honoured a power greater than themselves, they were humble to their own soul, to higher guidance, and they all listened to their deepest voice, their inner voice and obeyed. And they were forever students of life. They were humble to others too.

"Contentment – everything you want, you already got. It's a mindset of abundance nothing can be missing -- Abundance - no wanting."

Chapter 5. Harmony at Work

What humans call happiness and comfort, profit and gain (which is all some long for and wish to attain), is harmony. An object may be attained by either good or bad methods, yet still be obtained. But it is the way in which one attains that object that defines life as harmonious or not. Is not the object that is bad or good, it is the way in which one adopts or attains it that leaves an imprint on its form. All manner of dark force can obtain the object, but the darkness of it can never be removed. Disharmony is a virus that attaches to both the doer and the achievement. No one, no matter what their life looks like on the surface, can over come the darkness (karma) of their action. Greed and cruelty are toxins to the human heart and all suffering caused by it, comes back to haunt us.

Success in business is not absolutely dependent on harmony, but sustainable success is. Correct decisions, dealing with people, clear communication, intuition and analysis all work to their highest degree when there is integrity that comes from personal harmony - good intent.

Stay joyful.

A blind drive for achievement makes all the beauty around us turn to heaviness in our minds, bodies, and hearts. This pulls life and heart down-to-earth, and by that, everything becomes limited. When harmony is gone all sense of fun and play is gone. The child within has no room to breathe, tension mounts and humour is lost. We often try to achieve without the essential rhythm of harmony. Ignorance can build assets but it cannot sustain them. Wealth can build a fortress but how does it feel to live there? Ironically, there is no need to expend such energy, because success, wealth and abundance are the natural principles of a harmonious life. To flow with nature's laws, you can have both abundance and harmony - they are intrinsically connected.

Offices harmony and products.

Colour impacts thought. Mess impacts thought. Open plan offices are a curse to the deeper psychic levels of mind. Disturbance is not just audible. Witnessing aggressive individuals one does not have to speak to them to be affected. Depression is the same. Pictures on wall and many other symbolic icons create an ambience, which can be psychically disturbing or positively conducive to deep, creative inspirational work.

Ultimately, harmonics appeal to a unique part of the mind. The environment in an office can create or destroy harmony. For example, red walls excite a person and will make them inclined to fight. A striking colour will give you an argumentative environment. Bright white torments the mind. Black sedates it. Green opens us and blue is creative and expansive. This is a whole life science and one that is vital to harmonious environments.

Products reflect the mindset of the people who make them. Consider the manufacturer of ships and planes and other methods of transportation that are used daily. Who makes these vehicles? Who knows what suffering or internal struggles existed in the minds of those who built the Titanic? Was there a peacemaker amongst them, coaching them to keep a certain rhythm of mind while making the great ship? Were the individuals who handled each and every beam distracted and impatient, or were they living in harmony and presence? Everything that is made carries an influence in it. If a vehicle is made with thought that is contrary to what is required for it to run smoothly, then surely it will show in mechanical failure or bad luck.

In short, there is thought attached to all things prepared either by an individual or by a multitude, and that thought must give and cause results.

Products – secret meaning.

Our current lifestyles do not foster an appreciation for the energy and love put into products, and we carelessly purchase items without much thought. There was a time, in both Eastern and Western countries, when people would spend significant amounts of time preparing clothes, incorporating ritual and tradition in the process of creating a garment. Now an article can be easily bought at a shop and many people don't consider where or by whom it is made: whether it was made grudgingly or with grumbling. If a garment is made with love and affection, then the owner will feel supported in their pursuits while they wear the clothing. This is a powerful communication without form.

When shopping, hold an item, close your eyes, and trust that instinct. When you have to ask, "should I or shouldn't I buy this?" You know your heart is closed to it. Its true value is worthless. If on the other hand you are obsessed by it, then your judgement is impaired; you are blinded. Objects have an energy, a harmonic.

When you buy them, inherit them or receive and give them, you inherit the energy of the giver, the maker the creator of the thing. Be mindful where something has come from.

Writing.

Before writing any communication be conscious to become thankful. In this state the most accurate message will be conveyed.

In writing a letter, the author may sometimes mask the true meaning, yet the letter conveys all the messages that have not been written. People say that emails are easy to misinterpret, but I don't think so. I think people really feel the energy behind an email, careless or loving, appreciation or criticism flows through the system and people react.

Words written with living thoughts behind them will have a far greater effect than a thousand pages of dry, well written literature. Have you ever "heard" a letter speaking? It is not simply what is written on the paper, a letter brings the person who wrote it to life. You can decipher the mood they were in, their pleasure, their displeasure, their joy and their sorrow. A letter carries the vibration of thought and feeling, as do all forms of communication. And it is this vibration that can again surface long after the words and content of the communication have lost their meaning.

There are written words that emanate the vibration of their authors. Some of these great texts are the Koran, the Bible, the Darma, the Bhagavagita and more. The words in these books express a greater message than the words that are written. It is what is found between the lines that speak to us. The messages will grow and spread into your being and evolve you. They will touch you deep in your core and you will know it.

The power that lies in a book is not only in reading the words but the energy that surrounds them. In New York there is a Library called The JP Morgan Library. It is an awe-inspiring library, filled with hundreds of antique bibles that are stored in racks. The power of the space not only comes from Morgan himself, and how he has created such a mystical, powerful space, but from the books and their own secret energy from thousands of years gone by.

Brands and names.

Names have a psychic effect upon their owners and even upon their surroundings. The sacred names of God, the holy names of the prophets and saints, are written according to the law of their numerical value. And by the combination of such names, written or repeated in certain numerical form, wonders are performed.

The meaning of a name has great influence upon its possessor as well as upon others. From the sound of the letter and the word they compose, the mystic can understand much about the fate of a person. For example, vowels play a great part in the name and its influence. "E" and "I" are the feminine qualities of grace, wisdom, beauty and receptivity. "O" and "U" denote masculine qualities of power and expression. "A", sits between the masculine and feminine, it is the centre, the core around which all spoken words revolve. Thus vowels, in the composition of a name, also have an effect according to their place within the name Their placement serves to create a rhythm and rhythm has a meaning all of it's own.

Rhythm will also create meaning in the way in which a name begins and how it ends, whether evenly or unevenly. The rhythm of the name suggests the main thing in life balance or its lack thereof. Lack of balance is a deficiency in character, and causes adversity in life.

Many people have changed their lives by changing their names.

For example the Christian name has greater influence than the surname, as the effect of the name is proportional to its frequency of use. Shortened names such as Bill for William will lessen the effect of the name. The names given by the parents have a double effect, that of the name itself and that of the will of the one who gave it. There are many instances where a change of name has brought an entire change to a person's life.

The effect that a person's name has on them has a great deal to do with his or her life. The vibration of a name permeates the mind-body connection and sinks deeply into the consciousness. If this is so, then what effect does every word that one speaks in each day of a full lifetime have upon our surroundings and us?

Chapter 6. Harmony of Things

We have spoke at length about Personal Harmony and dealt with the inner environment. Now we must look to the outer because it is equally important. Harmony shows itself in objects and places. There are many ancient places where one can discover engraved stones, woods carved with artistic designs, or some symbolic representation of an ancient people's prayers. I have found such places while trekking in the mountains of Nepal, where one finds miles of Mani stones, engraved over thousands of years by a people steeped in their commitment to prayer.

A person who is blessed with the gift of intuition can read these vibrations. Outwardly, things may appear solid, but inwardly they are a narrow continual record, a talking record that is always expressing what is written within it, where it has been, and the energy that has surrounded it. No traveller with an attunement to their intuition will deny the fact that in lands of ancient traditions, you will experience numerous places which sing aloud the legends of their past.

The same experience can be found in the atmosphere of trees in the forest. They also express the past and the ancient impressions that have been given to them by those who sat amongst them. Often, people have superstitions about a tree being haunted, especially in the East. In truth, someone who has lived there or taken shelter under the tree has created a vibration, consciously or unconsciously. Their ponderings, thoughts or feelings have been absorbed into the tree and the tree's vibration expresses it. The tree is still repeating the thought that has been passed on to it. The tree can express the voice that has spoken to it with more clarity because it is a pure, uncontaminated container.

In those countries where people once travelled long distances by foot through the forests and took shelter under certain trees, such trees are rich in messages and questions. Many aboriginal cultures adhere to this system of communication, seeking answers from the wisdom of the trees or even rocks. With highly developed intuitive faculties, they will hear the messages more clearly than if they had heard them from a living person.

Art–Objects – Things carrying a deep impact.

In a creative work of art there also exists a perceptible feeling that comes from it, of it, independent of the skill required to produce the piece and the ideas it conveys to us. In every picture, in every statue, in every artistic construction, one can hear the voice within the piece, telling the story of its purpose, the workings of the mind of the artist, and the reason for its creation. Sometimes an artist is unaware of their purpose for creating their work, they may be just following their imagination. There may be a result that contradicts their desired image, or there may be a product that tells a greater message than what they were aware of during its creation.

A friend once took me to see paintings made by his wife. When I saw them I was able to read the whole history of her life. It was obvious that his wife had experienced severe depression and was living outside her body. The pain of her story was expressed in the vibrations of those paintings. As much as the paintings expressed angelic pictures of the life ever after, a fine thread of sadness and depression weaved itself through the pictures. Whoever now owns those paintings will surely feel the vibration of a life not fully lived. You can see this not by looking with your eyes, because eyes are blind to feeling, you can see it with your heart. Consciously or unconsciously –the energy of these paintings will permeate the life of their owner. They may admire their purchase, boast at the investment, yet, their life, and lives of their family who share the environment of this art will be affected regardless.

Animals absorb the vibrations of their owner.

Communication can be found among animals as well. Pets absorb thought and feeling through their contact with their owners, humankind. Those who know horses are very particular in buying one, which has good vibrations (apart from considering its health and breed). Often a horse of very good breed and perfectly sound health can be unlucky. The reason for this is that the disposition of its former rider will have been left in the energy of the animal, leaving its influence on the heart of the horse. Perhaps the personality of the person will change, but the horse will express behaviours indicative of the time spent with its previous owner.

Harmony of design - space.

Be mindful of design elements that are not harmonious. A staircase in the wrong place, a chair, a table doors placed in wrong areas break the harmonics, mathematics of space. The Ancient Greeks were fanatical about proportion defining love as symmetry, proportion and order.

The Greek mysteries included in their doctrines the magnificent concept of the relationship existing between harmony and form applied to elements. Architecture, for example, was considered comparable to musical notes, or as having a musical counterpart. Consequently when a building was erected in which a number of these elements were combined, the structure was then likened to a musical chord, which was harmonic when it fully satisfied the mathematical requirements of harmonic intervals. The realization of this analogy between sound and form led Goethe to declare that "architecture is crystallized music."

In constructing their temples of initiation, the early priests frequently demonstrated their superior knowledge of the principles underlying harmonics. A considerable part of the mystery rituals consisted of invocations and intonements, in special sound chambers. A word whispered in one of these compartments was so intensified that the reverberations made the entire building sway and be filled with a deafening roar. The very wood and stone used in the erection of the sacred buildings eventually became so thoroughly permeated with the sound vibrations of these religious ceremonies that when struck they would reproduce the same tones revealing that harmony becomes impressed into substances through ritual.

Surround yourself with harmony.

Surround yourself with a home, a place, of business, furniture, literature, music, art, people, various articles, conditions and atmospheres all things that conform with the idea and that tend to keep the perfection in mind and exercise a silent influence in agreement upon mind and body.

Create an environment of love, acceptance and intensity. Build joy and abundance. Create sacred space in all areas in which you create your life. Home office, wherever. These environments secretly speak to you, they create the future. Therefore, the arrangement of furniture, the placement of mirrors, vases, walls and doors, all must be done in the context of harmony. Each piece has its vibration. It's keynote. And the combination of symmetry proportion and order of the space and the furniture and fittings creates the harmonic of a space.

Be Aware of the history of the home or office you live in. Past trauma and ill will can infest a home or office. Sometimes for the life of that place. Be ware of the Real Estate Sales person who offers the idea of a makeover to change the feel of a place. It is usually deeper than that.

Artefacts.

There is a trend to transport ancient artefacts from one culture to the next and sell these as home decorations. I strongly advise to be careful what you buy, because owning some of these religious artefacts is like drinking poison. Items of religious significance stolen from their home become dark shadows in the home of the innocent buyer. Rarely do artefacts of significant heritage leave their origin with the permission of the ancient owners – you cannot be too careful about the level of psychic influence.

The thought that accompanies an object is a vibration of free energy, a life energy. The vibrations passed into an object are neither audible nor visible; they are only perceptible by feeling. You may wonder to what they are perceptible? They become perceptible to the inquisition. This is not to say that one who lacks intuition cannot perceive such vibrations, rather, they will do so unconsciously.

Gifts.

Harmony exists in all things. Inside every object hides a thought and this thought becomes the message –irrespective of the nature of the object. The message in-turn will find its home. For example, the flowers one takes to a patient in the hospital can convey our healing thoughts. The patient will receive whatever messages we passed along each time they look at the flowers. Therefore every little thing given and taken in love, with a harmonious and good thought, has a greater value than the object itself. It becomes evident to us then, that it is not simply the everyday tasks of our life to hold and create material value, but also to focus on the source of our motivation, our thoughts and our integrity. It is our thoughts that are projected into the world, through the creations that hold our energy. We can choose to pass on negative destructive thoughts or harmonious, constructive thoughts. When we are mindful of the harmony of our thinking and therefore our creations, at all times, then we can watch our work become a thousand times greater in effect and value.

Music that heals.

Many ancient Greeks were known to have used harmonics, through music, to cure disease. Pythagoras himself cured many ailments of the spirit, soul and body and mind. Having certain specially prepared musical compositions played in the presence of the sufferer or by personally reciting short selections from such early poets as Hesiod and Homer. In their university at Crotona it was customary for the Pythagoreans to open and close the day with songs -- those in the morning calculated to clear the mind from sleep and inspire the activities of the day; those in the evening were of modes soothing, relaxing and conducive to rest.

"Having once established harmony as an exact science, Pythagoras applied his newly found law of harmonic intervals to all the phenomena of nature, even going so far as to demonstrate the harmonic relationship of the planets, constellations, and elements to each other. Pythagoras concluded that the laws of harmony were determined, not by the sense perceptions of the human body, but by reason and mathematics. Then he totally recognized the profound effect of music upon the senses and emotions, he did not hesitate to use harmony to influence the mind and the body with what he termed, "musical medicine". A good example is the story of a young man who, with broken heart, decided to burn the house of his unfaithful girlfriend. A flutist was playing a fast and excited tune nearby, which, in Pythagoras eyes was exciting the young man's frenzy. Pythagoras asked the flutist to change the music to reflect harmonics, slow and rhythmic music and with this the young man abandoned his frenzy and returned home."

Plato depreciated the notion that music was intended solely to create cheerful and agreeable emotions, maintaining rather "it should evoke a love of all that is noble, a rejection of all that is mean, and that nothing could be more strongly influence man's innermost feelings and melody, than harmony and rhythm."

The Greek initiates also recognized a fundamental relationship between the individual, the heavens, and harmony. They used the seven sacred vowels, and so words became sacred. Pythagoreans believed that "everything which existed had a voice and all creatures were eternally singing the praise of the creator. Man fails to hear these divine melodies because he is enmeshed in the illusion of material existence (mind). When he liberates himself from the bondage of the lower world with its sense limitations, the music of the spheres will again be audible as it was in the golden age. Harmony recognizes harmony, and when the human soul regains its true state it will not only hear the celestial choir but will also join with it in an everlasting anthem of praise to that eternal good."

Language.

Every word we speak and every syllable we hear has an affect upon the body through the power of their vibration. For thousands of years, medicine relied on the concepts of vibration found inside and outside the body to determine wellness and cure disease. This technique was lost over time, but there has been an increasingly growing awareness of the healing power of vibrations.

Not only do words greatly affect the body, but they also affect the mind. For instance, if a person is called "foolish" time and time again, they will, eventually, become foolish. If we call a simple person wise, in time they will become wise. A child, who grows up hearing judgment and being told they are incapable, comes to believe that as truth. On the other hand, a child who makes mistakes and is encouraged to keep trying, affirmed for small victories, learns to take risks and set high goals.

A person who speaks about their illness nourishes their illness by speaking about it. It is sad to hear people speak like this, because their perceived reality is far from the truth. The emotional perceptions we have invade our reality and become the illusions we begin to believe. Subconscious thought (which determines our attitude) and conscious awareness play an equally important role in the development and unfolding of our lives.

Each word we speak is accompanied by another world. This hidden world both reflects, and manifests, its outcome. A person who is insincere can mask such a message with their choice of words, but the insincerity is revealed on a different level. The vibration and inclination of the voice will secretly betray any lies or falsehoods. We are given the clear message of a lie but the person behind the mask is the one who suffers.

In truth, it is not the word itself that is so powerful, but the feeling and vibration that the word creates. Some words attract power, some bring release from difficulties, and some give courage and strength. There are simple words and there are secret words that are more powerful still. When a person in need of peace and rest uses words that bring courage and strength, they will become even more restless. Words with negative, angry and bitter tones, if spoken enough, can affect the physiological make up of the body. In contrast, certain songs, poems, and speeches, whether by intent or by circumstance, have become renowned in the healing process for helping people. Grief can be released and soothed with the uttering of specific words.

It is not always what we say, but how we feel it, how we express it, and what power is hidden behind our expression. Two people might speak the same truth, yet one is believable while the other is not. What is the difference? It is the vibration that is different. The individual's personal story is different, therefore their beliefs are different, and their thinking is different. One has conviction the other is repeating knowledge.

The atmosphere contains the power of our thoughts. People admire cool self-possessed presentation; they dislike active nervous people who try to carry everything before them as a storm. Coolness allows us to be most powerful by allowing us to think more rapidly, carrying more intensity and concentration in thought. The harmonious person proceeds easily. Words are well chosen, spoken carefully, the audience listens, the language is interesting, it shows thought, care in preparation and belief in its declarations.

Chapter 7. Your Life Force

People search for Harmony for many reasons. But the most basic one is to be free of the tension.

Infinite volumes of spiritual literature can be reduced to a few simple choices in life. Either to be consumed by tensions, or to rise above them. It is really that simple. Tensions that consume our life are bondage. They lead us to live a reactionary existence and represent our inability to immerse ourselves in life with integrity.

In everyday life we act out our choices. The depth of our commitment to our personal harmony shows in many ways. We demonstrate the reality of our own motivations through our interactions with other people and through the quality of the environment we create. It is important for us to understand this so that we can look at ourselves in a realistic way and begin to make our choices, with consciousness.

Understand that how you deal with tensions, yours and others is really the fulcrum point. It is the daily articulation of your understanding of service, of love and respect. It is a practical and powerful expression of real love and respect to take the tensions, both your own and others, and to deal with them. As you cultivate this love and respect you are developing a powerful self-mastery, which you articulate in your genuine capacity to serve other human beings. Finally, it is a no jive, no frills down to earth, real life expression that you can do every single day. In this effort of consuming tensions lie the nourishment and the fuel necessary for the total transformation that you ask for: personally and globally.

We have this opportunity to choose many times each day. We can make the effort to be open and to live with a genuine love and respect for ourselves and for others; we can choose to see all our inner effort as an investment in the quality of our outer life. We can choose this or we can let ourselves be consumed by doubts, fears, judgments, anger, worries and insecurities. You have to choose your outcome carefully. Instead of being consumed by tension you can instead open yourself and feel the flow of that energy pass through you and you grow as a result. Then you become free, free of all the biological, psychological, and emotional restrictions that endlessly limit human beings to an unfortunately stupid and harsh existence.

This is habitual conditioning and it is what truly keeps us from living our true nature. So much of it is unconscious and socialized: The hunger for wealth, the fear of death, the fear of loneliness, the sense of insignificance. These are socialized responses to normal life. So we have choices. Listen to the ego and therefore identity and operate in fear and uncertainty or follow the heart and operate without reason but with security.

To live with self-awareness is not just meditating: although this can release tensions and reactions. It is really about becoming aware of the essence of your own life, and then beginning to live from that essence, whether you're walking, riding the subways, working in your job, or something else. Personal harmony comes from being aware of that essence at all times. Then whether you're sitting still or moving around is irrelevant. You wont need a special place – environment in order to have that experience. You will have expended the experience of all the techniques into your whole life, and made your whole life itself an act of meditation.

Find and secure daily stillness – Mind - Body - Spirit.

"Quiet the mind means to isolate the mind. Still the mind means to go somewhere deeper. Quiet the mind is vulnerable. It is the surface of the lake always ready for something to disturb its surface. Still the mind means to dive beneath the surface of the lake. Where surface ripples do not disturb the stillness."

All we need to do is find a way of being still in the world so that even if the sun rose in the west instead of the East we would still follow the same path.

The robber entered the house of the monk. It was early morning and the monk was sitting in meditation. The monk saw the robber as he lifted a priceless vase from the shelf. The monk, frightened the robber and said "sir, please be careful with the vase when you take it, you know it is very valuable." When the robber, holding tight to his sword moved closer, the monk said "if you are looking for money, it's in the jar over there, but please leave the five notes for my taxes tomorrow." Puzzled and grateful the robber left, with vase and money well hidden. Next day, everybody in the village was in turmoil because many people were also robbed that night. Then someone noticed that the priceless vase was missing from the monk's hearth, they went into shock. "Oh no, the precious vase is stolen" The monk replied calmly, "No, no, I wasn't robbed." "No, last night I gave the vase to a stranger, along with some money, he thanked me and left. He was pleasant enough fellow, but a little careless with his sword."

"The resolution is to be without disturbance to my own mind or to the repulsion of others to do this one thing splendidly, satisfactorily- a determination to achieve the support of others through attraction to achieve my desire."

Nervous tension – Kills harmony.

Disharmony and exhaustion occurs when vital energy is thrown away by the erratic action of the nervous system. Emotion, stress and nervous tension are the greatest leakage of personal life force known to mankind. No physician, no medicine, no drugs, pills or electric treatments have been able to stop leakage of personal life force and the loss of vitality caused by excess emotional tension, nervous tension and stress.

Harmony can be acquired. And it is an attractive force. It is simply achieved by breaking the habits of the body, regulating thoughts, steadiness of the eye and calming the mind. (Emotional stability) Add techniques of breathing and graceful, steady poise and you have created magnetic attraction of the highest order.

Disharmony is one of the greatest causes of loss of vitality, and is a repelling energy. It is reflected in the person who is uneasy, fidgety, squirming or in any other way addicted to irritated activity. Restlessness is bad a habit. It is the cause of lost vitality, lost concentration, lost focus, lost clarity and is the primary generator of mental diseases such as depression. Steadiness is an art that should be taught to children. The harmonious and attractive person is not restless and is magnetic to others.

Self control – Mindful action – Sustains harmony within.

Freedom from restlessness is not stiffness or fixed position. Relaxation is the basis of ease, polish and grace. There is a power in correct relaxation and it is certainly not slough or laziness.

Uncontrolled bodily movements such as the frequent change of position, the moving of arms, legs, hands, fingers, eyelids, mouth, face muscles and various twitching, jerkiness indicate chronic nervous energy waste. This is when muscular energy is runaway without purpose and without control. Preventing physical leakage paves the way for new and life giving vitality. Steadiness is a habit. To bring poise into your life and relationship, become observant to all unnecessary motion you make and reduce your movements. Self-mastery inspires confidence in others, thus increasing success. Powerful people are deep. The stronger the feelings, the less should be their outward evidence.

- The fidgeter makes you uneasy. You'll have no confidence in a person who fidgets. Restless people make all around uneasy. Restless people cannot become magnetic.

- Fidgeting. Especially with the fingers, tapping, scratching, moving around, odd movements of the arms and fingers reveal an unconscious deterioration in presence and vitality. This also applies to feet swinging under the table or tapping on the floor. Fingers feet hands feet drumming are all reflections of leakage in vitality.

- Posture. Sitting position, slouching in a chair, head resting in the hands, leaning back, lounging, shoulders hunched, spine compressed. Short breathing is a negative habit that invites mouth open breathing and this is injurious to health. Sighing induces depression and sadness – both demagnetize the body.

- Nervous reaction is a construction of the mind. Nervous shock drives out more vital energy than can be stored in days of steady behaviour. Sudden starts affect the whole body or a part of it. Trembling, like unsteady movements, reflect weakness of nerves and mind. Halting speech sucks energy. One in 200 people talk without halting. The cure for this is to speak smoothly by direction of the will. Rapid talk also drains energy, as excess talk does. Nervous exhaustion is the penalty of the person who talks too much and too fast.

Mental health a powerful key to Personal Harmony and vitality.

Disharmony in life occurs primarily because of worry. Examine your speech for negative terms, look to your creative output for opportunities to improve.

Physicians say that more vitality is lost, and most people die from mental stress, worry. Worry lessens the energy of every part of the body - mind, nervous system, the functions of the organs, the power of digestion, the power of accurate thinking, the respiration and the circulation. The most dangerous and the most prolific cause of nervous breakdown is worry. Worry is a mental disease that is like a cancer. Melancholy is also caused by worry.

When your mind is calm you feel in control. Peace of mind builds personal power. When your mind is calm and your body is relaxed, your immune system and therefore your health is at a peak. When you honour your body, it is in a relaxed and alert state so that focus and concentration are possible. You will radiate that vibrancy and vitality that attracts the investment of other people in your purpose and vision. Clarity and certainty will be reflected in your appearance and speech.

"If you have less energy at the end of the day than at the beginning, you've got bad stress."

Beyond inner conflict - Reconnecting the heart and mind.

"Whatever makes a person more valuable to himself will make him more valuable to others. Personal improvement lifts the individual up through thoughts, ideas, impulses and by keeping the company of inspired souls. From this habit of looking onward and upward, comes the spirit of initiative. It is an amazing training, always looking for ways of betterment. It is valuable in any area of your life."

How can I relax if I am always comparing the way I am to some confused ideal? If I feel bad and yet hold the belief that I should not feel bad, then I feel doubly bad.

We create patterns, devices, to help us avoid confronting our beliefs. We create, ideals, self-image. I have witnessed the journey of many young people who commit suicide because of the contradiction between the reality of their life and their self-image. This self-image comes from knowledge. This knowledge is rarely the knowledge of truth but some belief system that has been handed to them through experience, observation or education.

Our responses can be divided into two groups, wise and unwise, or skilful or unskillful.

The unwise group – emanate from the "lower self" they experience as fear, hatred aversion, greed, attachment, hate, doubt, and jealousy. When we are in this mode we are in reaction to the world. These are strategies of aversion, fear, protection, and they lead to unhappiness because each has an opposite.

The wise group emanate from the "higher self": love, wisdom, joy, equanimity, and confidence. They are natural states that do not result from knowledge or experience. The training is an openness that goes beyond the lower sense of our self.

Unhealthy response is: Grasping mind.

Built on insufficiency, the "if only" mind which works on the premise that "If only I had that – and if only I had this" – all would be OK. This wanting mind, wanting to be filled. Always looking at the world to see what they want. Always thinking – what else do I want tomorrow. The result is a sad and painful existence.

Unhealthy response is: Aversion mind.

Built on resistance push away, the judge and avoidance mind. It's always looking for what's wrong, looking to negate. Always looking at the world to see what they don't want. Always thinking – "what don't I like about this." It's a sad and painful existence.

Unhealthy response is: Delusion.

Always confused, what should I do, what's this all about mind. This person is always dragging their feet, always uncertain. This mind always has too many options, too many choices, fear rules it. This mind is always looking at the world waiting for the right answer hoping something or someone will know or guide them. Always thinking, panic, and anxiety – it's a sad and painful existence.

Unhealthy response is: Fear mind.

Drives a sense of smallness and therefore generate strategies for safety in life. These unskillful strategies for life are ways that have been taught, learned or borrowed from others; the person with the grasping mind says get more, more and more to be safe. The person with the aversion mind says -- resist it and it will be safe. The person with the deluded mind, says ignore it, ignore it, stay uncommitted and it will be safe. But none are true.

"A Monk once said – I don't understand the west you don't want what you have – and you want what you don't have. Why not change it. Why not want what you have and don't want what you don't have. Then you can be happy. How do we come to peace with life, including its challenges?"

Chapter 8. Learn to Unlearn Harmony Comes from This

In this chapter we look at ways to shift your mindset to guarantee happiness and personal harmony stay with you throughout your life. It means being willing to shift your thinking, every now and then.

"Spirituality and Harmony does not come from analysing the past. It comes from releasing it. "

It is said in the east that the first thing to be learned is to unlock what has already been learned and then unlearn it. This unlearning is what is called real knowledge, wisdom. Knowledge is learned from the outside – wisdom comes from within. In other words, we have to learn how to become a good student, to let go easily. To see a person and say, "that person is bad", is learning. To see further, and recognize something good in that person, is unlearning. When you see the goodness in someone you have already called bad, you have unlearned. You have see with two eyes. You learn by seeing with one eye; then you unlearn and see with two eyes. This makes the learning complete. It requires humility, being humble. It means losing our individuality, that individuality which has been collected and accumulated. To surrender in the awareness that one's ideas and opinions are just a collection of erroneous facts that, through conditioning or experience have been adopted as truth? They are simply collections of data and knowledge that need to be unlearned.

How can one unlearn all these stories that have been collected in a lifetime? It is said by some that the personality is engraved on the mind (and hence, that things cannot be unlearned). But I heartily disagree. For the sake of humanity, we all need to disagree. What we can do is add truth to half-truth. What has been learned is possibly only half the truth; we need to add the rest. Rather than take away, it means to unlearn is to add the missing pieces. Like a child learns by being open, but an adult learns, and locks onto that knowledge and no longer remains open to add more. They say, I know about you. But this is half learning.

Break cycles – Letting go of old Patterns.

The degree to which it's possible for a person to change from unproductive responses to productive responses is extraordinary. It requires a decision that going over the old pattern is too tiring and you are willing to make the effort to go someplace different.

This takes a serious commitment. Not a heavy commitment but a real determination. It all has to do with your willingness to control your own energy. This commitment doesn't require doing a lot of big things; instead it's the simple things that, together, are the most effective. These simple things are the little moments in-between, when you slowly build a different pattern. Like anything that you practice, if you try to be simple and regular about this every day, then you take the steam out of the big moment and the blow up points become less critical.

This is not talking about a different philosophy and dogma. Whether you are Hindu, Jewish, Muslim, a Christian or a Buddhist it makes no difference. The real people behind those philosophies are the same. So we don't speak to religion or earth bound philosophy, because this is only dealing with the personas, we talk to the real person behind the mask. This is the way we begin to break the cycles in your life. It begins and ends with a new story of the past events. We ask, "Can you see both sides of everything that has happened to you? Can you see that there was never a pain without pleasure, an upper without downer, a support without challenge"? It's very confronting, but essential in order to truly renew yourself and live in the future.

To break patterns something must change and it is within our deepest thinking that we will find the source of that change. In order to unravel the delusion that is the cause we must open our minds like children and this is very vulnerable for some people. This is why love transforms so much of life. If you are able to be in love you cannot hide. That is impossible. That is what people fear when they fear love. They fear being exposed. If you are in love it will show. Your eyes, your face, the way you walk, the way you sit, everything will show it, because you are not the same person. Harmony has come to your heart and it's perfectly natural.

When stories of righteousness abound, people self-destruct. Healing, growth and advancement are retarded. You can't heal a depression and think the same thoughts after it. In fact, it is not what you think that causes depression but how you think. Changing how we think, both as an individual and in nations, confronts the old conventions. If there is any story about your past, that holds a positive without a negative, a support without a challenge, a good without a bad, a right without a wrong, anything that is not in perfect balance, you are going to live that story over and over and over until you get to grow out of it.

Truth – Seek the balance in all things.

To break a pattern, to change an addiction, we must revisit the past with the eye of a detective. How could there be a good without a bad? How could I be missing something? How could there be an event in my life that was not part of universal law? In other words out of balance. What event, person, place or thing am I not thankful for? Here are the keys to the great unravelling of knowledge, and the true learning - unlearning, to obtain freedom and wisdom. It is therefore by way of stillness, being alone and the adjustment of perceptions of the past, that we can change what our memory holds; then we can add real thinking instead of half truth to our mind, we sleep well at night with this perspective, a universal one. With this skill, we can let go the past and move on.

There is nothing in the universe that is out of balance and most importantly this includes your real stories. Any story from the past that holds more pain than pleasure or more pleasure or pain – needs to be unlearned, it is a lie. Any story that holds a good without a bad is another lie. Any story that does not conclude with a thank you; is running your life. Your perceptions of events however may not be so clear. That's learning, perceptions say, "that one was good and that one was bad." But perceptions are received in the most impure environments, when fear and anxiety may have filtered fact.

So the question is, are you living the past over and over again, or are you living renewed every day of your life. How can dreams come true if you keep repeating the same life over and over? If you don't change what you think, you create the same things you created yesterday. That is the most obvious truth. Today was created by yesterdays thinking and today's thinking creates tomorrow's reality. Unless something changes today then tomorrow must be the same as yesterday.

How much of life you can see the balance in – it's simple really.

Changing stories of the past.

Harmony is perfect balance. But fears, anger and every other emotion thrive on imbalanced thoughts. The ego thrives on imbalanced thoughts; it cannot exist without imbalanced thought, better worse, competitive mind states. Strange how sometimes the competitive spirit drives the most materially successful people.

Fear, approval, inadequacy drove them their whole life to try to prove something. The drive made results but the real ambition was never fulfilled, self love, and personal harmony was not achieved. We can have both success and harmony.

Through seeing our past stories as a balance of pleasure and pain, good and evil, right and wrong, we learn to recognize move forward in life. False ego will say there was an event in the past that was good without bad or visa versa. But that is false. That is the ego, the false self. It is in this realization that we can comprehend the beauty of life. It is in this realization that we are born again, a birth that opens the doors to a future. Why would we hold back? To repeat those stories is to repeat the past. People who listen to our old stories are just making it harder for us to get on with life. It would be better if they refused to listen to old stories of self-pity.

Find the beauty in everything that has happened to you, find the blessing in every situation, find the gift that was created in the event and you will grow. You will expand beyond the narrow definition of yourself as a one sided being and learn what it is like to say, "there is nothing about me I need to change" you will find the beauty of your life and that of others and then you will forget shame and guilt and expectations that kill life, and be free to move into work and relationship with your true nature.

Your life must become a mirror of pure balance; you have to see the positive in every negative situation and the negative in every positive situation. This means a refusal to become one-sided, learning to never make a stand, because with a universal perspective you understand that everything in this world is in perfect balance and therefore to stand on one side or the other is self-destructive.

Fear of letting go – Seeking abundance.

We only hold onto the past because we think the future holds no hope, it's a lack of abundance. We stay attached to people, places and stories because we fear, that in the future, there can never be anything as good as, as happy as, as kind as, as loving as, as bad as the past. The person who lives in the past lives in fear of the future. Small problems become big stress, this is how they stay in the past, and they refuse to move on.

The person who is stuck in the past will be meagre. They will be tight, ungenerous and self focused because they fear loss. Ultimately, you will know those who are stuck in the past: they are the ones who are most attached, to people, places, things and stories.

Abundance comes from a universal perspective, and from this vantage, there is no wanting. There is nothing to change. Nothing is missing, just changed in form. Then there is no holding on for everything that we release will appear in a new form, instantaneously.

You'll need confidence in the future to be abundant. In the human condition there can be a lot of insufficiency, and therefore desire; and out of this desire is born a particular mode of life or a method of action which keeps us from fully experiencing life in the present. We struggle for improvement day after day and therefore are never content. Never satisfied. It is the drive built from insecurity and insufficiency. With this mindset, this reaching out there must be conflict; there must be misery and a sense of shallowness and emptiness and of the utter futility of life. What is gained is feared to be lost. Like reaching out for a feather, the more we grope and grasp the further away it goes. Insufficiency means we seek from the outside world what must already exist within.

By the laws of nature, nothing is missing. There is no insufficiency. Nothing is missing it just changes in form. It's universal. So there can be no wanting from a universal viewpoint. Nothing is missing in anyone's life, it just changes in form.

Nothing is ever missing – it just changes in form.

The attachment to form can ruin our lives. When a father dies while the child is young. The child may claim and then spend the whole of their life acting out the consequence; "my father died when I was young," they may say. We can have great compassion for their experience. But is it the truth from a universal viewpoint. From a universal perspective, the father did not die - he was not missing. Like a house that burned to the ground, he was not in his body, the form is gone, the house is now in atoms and dust, but he is not gone. We grieve the old form. We are very attached to having things appear in our lives the way we want them. Actually, the whole story is a myth; in truth even those things we thought were missing are not missing.

You can examine this. One lady in a seminar said, "My father died when I was a child and I have had relationship problems my whole life" So I asked, "what was it that you missed about him?" It was very painful for her, but she had motivation to do the work, her life was really in a mess and the man she loved was leaving her and the children. She answered with 100 things, like "his confidence, his advice, his friendship, his security, his strength, his guidance, his eyes, his hands, his voice his love and more and more."

If nature abhors a vacuum, then nothing can be missing. I asked her, "then, I know he was passed but in what form did these parts of your father still exist?" for example "his confidence – who, came into your life to replace that missing element? She remembered her brother stepped in to do that more. And his touch? - "my mother." You will find everything step by step the whole story will become strangely transparent. "And who came into your life to fill the void of his advice?" and you will find it. Sometimes the individual themselves took over that missing element but very often it is a new friend or old associate who steps in. Nothing is missing; every single thing that was seen missing was there. It is all a story.

And then she ran out of things that were missing. She was very angry now because her whole personality was based on this story and in such a short time, after 10 years in therapy, the whole story was gone. And now I asked "so what is missing" and she said "nothing, I just wanted to tell my daddy that I loved him" tears were running down her cheeks and mine and everyone because it was love that was coming from her now, not pain. I said, "close your eyes, who do you feel standing behind you right now, who do you feel with their hand on your shoulder?" she burst into tears and there was no mind games anymore, there were no words anymore, just love and she spoke to him, in front of 100 people, and everyone was in tears because that was real. All her pain was that she forgot to say, "I love you."

This lady was very brave. Not only that but she was a Native American woman and she was really going against her culture doing this work in a conference room. After the loving tears went away, she looked 10 years younger, she had a big open face and love was there. She was in the present for the first time in a lot of years.

The fathers' love was not lost; it was and is always there in the heart of the child. Once you get past the insufficiency, the idea that something was missing, then there is nothing to block the love and there is nothing missing. Any person who goes through this process will feel the presence of the "missing person" once they feel that nothing is missing.

Do what you love.

When your emotions override your inspirations, when your body mind becomes over stimulated or depressed, when you are not doing what your love, you dissipate and waste your life force. If every human is gifted by nature with an identical amount of this energy then the first step in taking responsible personal steps in life are to stop the losses of it.

Rest.

"Life moves not on a straight line but in rhythmic curves."

The harmonic person knows how to rest. As a matter of fact few people know anything about it. It is a very valuable art. There are those whose sleep is good but it is not psychically harmonizing. The harmony of sleep comes from a psychic state of peace and oneness, freedom from care and a receptive attitude toward life force that results in vital and attractive powers.

Before going to sleep at night you should:

- Be at Peace!
- Assume oneness with the All
- Banish care from the mind
- Relax muscles and nerves
- Think, easily, calmly, confidently "I shall this night develop magnetic power in every part of the body"
- And pauses, for a day or two, are especially important during the working of our regimes

True rest is restorative psychic activity. When the conscious mind is at peace within itself and with all existence then the subconscious knows that it can draw into the body the universal forces to rebuild and restore tissue and function.

"Humankind has made errors for ages - we've found supposed truths to be errors. One truth is succeeded by the next. Great religions arise and then better ones are born. The beings of today will change and so will those of tomorrow. The whole progress of man is a continuous agitation. The desire for constant conquest and change, and for success keeps raising us to higher and higher levels of stupidity. Surely, the price of unconscious disharmony is becoming too much to bare?"

Christopher Walker

So you can use the body mind to manage your life state. Open your spine to free your chest. Breath in balance, use the diaphragm. These are not exercises; these are habits. Sleep.

Sleep is also one of the greatest revitalizers we have. Most people habitually use stimulants and caffeine drinks that cause the nerves to be in an excited state and prevent the body from experiencing total rest and relaxation. When people discard their stimulants they become deep restful sleepers.

To relax yourself to sleep, first darken the room, turn off the TV or radio and lie flat on your back with your hands down by either side without touching your body, legs extended about a foot apart, head resting on a small pillow. Eyes remain open at first focusing on a point straight ahead of you. Gently slow your thoughts and allow your eyes to close. Avoid any interruptions and allow all muscles to completely relax.

No compromise – no excuses.

The outer environment, our mind, wants to crush the heart into this steel frame of standards, ideas, and edicts. The pressure comes from the outside and conflicts with the real you inside. Then there are excuses: I am doing it because of the baby, I am doing this because of being a good mother, I am doing it to be a good wife, I am doing it because, etc.

Naturally, when the mind is being twisted, shaped, perverted by outer environment, then there is a constant conflict within, a constant battle, constant false adjustments, the mind hopes for tranquillity, for happiness, by avoiding what is deep in the heart, there is always a resentment. Don't compromise your commitment to live in harmony with nature.

Expunge doubt.

Expunge doubt from your life. It forces friendship to the lowest level and creates uncertainty in all around you, and unpredictability in yourself.

In a search for harmony the emphasis is not on questioning but on doubt. This is significant because if you are asking intellectual questions, you are asking for a definite answer so that your problem can be dissolved. But you are really asking, let my doubts be cleared. And if you knew this you would not the asking them for answers, because the mind is always in doubt even after it has an answer it goes "I think there's more." Instead you would be asking for a transformation of your mind, because a doubting mind will remain at doubting mind no matter what the answers that are given to it. A doubting mind will remain a doubting mind no matter what intellectual knowledge is provided to it, the answers to the questions are really irrelevant. If you are given one answer and you have a doubting mind, you will doubt the answer. If you get another answer, and you have a doubting mind you will doubt that answer also. If you have a doubting mind, then a doubting mind means you will put a question mark on everything. To anything and everything that is presented to you, including love.

There was one man who woke up in a burning house. Someone yelled "fire - fire" – he woke and looked around in panic as flames began to engulf his home. He yelled "how did this happen? Why is the fire hot?" of course in the time he needed to get out he perished still trying to work out why.

How can doubts be cleared? Personal Harmony and contentment. It's not an idea; it's an experience.

"You must be the change you wish to see in the world."

Mahatma Gandhi

All of life is the result of your minds construction so you can likely choose the illusion or state of mind you wish to have. Why not, either you choose it or it is chosen for you. The extent to which you remain tangled up in your issues and therefore struggling is the extent to which your creative energy strangles in a self-destructive process.

Try instead to feel it in your heart, you can whistle a happy tune and find a reason to be thankful. Breathe into that sweetness. And continue to feel it circulate and expand until a real joy emerges. Breathe into that joy and start to allow a simple love of life to emerge within you. Then feel that, letting it flow inside of you – allow the simple love of life to emerge from within you. Then, feel that. Letting it flow within and around you.

Doing this can resolve everyone of your issues because doing that you no longer operate on the same level as the issues. Further more, when you really feel that fullness, then there's no longer any issue of anything being missing or of anything being there that shouldn't be. When you feel that fullness, you are in touch with your True Nature and completely responsible. Having dissolved the barriers to being happy, you become able to have a simple, pure and complete interchange with everything and everyone in your environment.

Today is the best day – Tomorrow never comes.

When I was a child my dad said, "If you work hard at school – you'll be happy." And then I took control and thought if I play sport, I'd be happy. Then I thought my girlfriend was the key to happiness. Then I got married and had children and I thought that was the key, and my business reached unbelievable heights of wealth and I thought that would make me happy. But the more those things made me happy the more I feared loosing them, and the more fear I had the unhappier I became. Then I thought spirituality would make me happy, and after 20 years I came to realize that it wouldn't. I think a lot of people live like this. And as they get very old they go to religion because they think when they die they'll be happy.

We have, deep down, the core ambition to be happy, all of us. We just apply different strategies to that path. "Hmm" they say, "this will make you happy," but really, after so much travel nothing of the sense makes you happy. Bending over backward in yoga does nothing for your real happiness.

Five friends were on a fishing trip. One man noticed a brass vase. They picked it up, rubbed it and hey presto a gene appeared. Each got a wish. The first wished for a case of beers, they arrived. The second wished for a beer factory. The first guy sighed in disappointment realizing the futility and waste of his small dream. The third guy then wished for a billion dollars. With it, he said, I will have a beer factory, a restaurant, a bar with dancers and a cure for my hangovers. The first two were saddened and depressed at the waste of their dreams. The forth guy learned form the first three. He immediately wished for three wishes. He ordered a billion dollars with the first wish, and the ice cream factory with the second and three more wishes with the third wish. The first three men were so depressed now; they began taking Prozac because they realized they could have done so much better. The fifth guy, wished for contentment. The first four stared at him in disbelief. "What"? They shouted in unison. "What?" He turned with a smile; his wealth was on his face, and in his heart, now he was happy with everything. "There is nothing I need, want or desire." He was free, and the wealthiest man of all.

"There are basically two paths to follow to happiness – freedom to desire and freedom from desire."

The very search for pleasure is the cause of suffering. Wanting to be other than where we are is the trigger for great pain and disturbance and accounts for much of all mental health problems that exist. There was a lady who had left her husband and was rebuilding her life. It had been two years of separation and she looked tired. She sat with me and shared the pain of her acrimonious divorce process. And it had been tough.

She said. "I am not happy. But when I sell my business, and then I don't have to work with those managers any more it will be different. And then I will sell my house and my boyfriend will move in and that will help me with my son. And then I can focus on my career and that will give me direction. And then I will not have to deal with my ex anymore. And I think I will move to the countryside and that will make it better." She wanted my help as a life coach to make this all happen for her. But all these achievements would not make any change in her life while she remained in the prison of her current thinking. The task became happiness before those things happened, not because of them.

"If we don't appreciate it the way that we've got it, we wont get it the way that we want it."

Summary.

When your emotions override your inspirations, when your body mind becomes over stimulated or depressed, when you are not doing what your love, you dissipate and waste vitality. If every human is gifted by nature with an identical amount of this energy then the first step in taking responsibility in life is to stop its loss. Tiredness, chronic fatigue, mental health, illness, and stress are all symptoms of the losses in personal harmony.

- Proper periods of rest.
- Variety of physical and mental action.
- Proper food and drink.
- Pure air.
- Physical cleanliness to assist elimination of waste.
- Regular activity of the muscles.
- Regular activity of the nerves.
- Regular activity of breathing.
- Regular exercise of the physical body.
- Healthy toned mental and emotional activity for the quickening of the brain centres.
- Proper clothing and favourable, healthful environments.
- High focus on purpose.
- Avoidance of excesses.
- Psychical and physiological harmony.

Chapter 9. Love Pockets in your Heart
Harmony in Your Relationships

It's easy to fall in love. That's nature's plan. God's plan. Falling in love is easy. Staying in love, well that's another topic all together.

Admit that you have a pocket in your heart for everyone you ever loved, sexed, danced with and that these pockets remain in your heart the whole of your life. There is nothing to let go of, just someone to love in a special love pocket in your heart. Then you'll see that loving life and partner is so easy because your heart is already filled with past loves all nicely placed in special pockets in your heart. If you have any darkness regarding someone you once loved, then that darkness fills that love pocket. You can also see that if you hate someone from the past, their little pocket in your heart has both love and toxic darkness in it and this explains your illness and current drama.

To keep those Love Pockets in your heart healthy, you must remind yourself that love is not an emotion; it is pure. There is no need to act on love, love is not an action; it is a lack of action. Love is everything but nothing; there is just beautiful, bright sunshine. You felt it before and you must feel it now for everyone you ever loved. Each person still lives within you, in a special heart pocket. There is no need to possess that person, the object of your love. In fact, pure love is to let them go. The end result of true love is to wish that person happiness, whether they are here or not. You can do your own "Love Pocket" test by thinking of all the people you ever knew and ask, "Do I feel warm, thankful and loving toward them?" If the answer is no, then panic, because they are still running your life and therefore ruining your health.

Only your ego is stopping you. Yes, the one who hurt you is the one you must love in order to raise your consciousness. Remember the earlier comment about "Unlearning" well here it is in real life terms. What you judged in someone you have to unlearn in order to evolve your consciousness. Nature destroys anything and anyone who does not fulfil their purpose. For the simplicity of this situation, the evolution of your consciousness is your purpose. Grow your love, change that ego, unlearn the judgements and refresh the "love pocket". Your life, health, lover and inspiration depend on it.

The sunshine that is love does not come to you. It is contained in these tiny love pockets in your heart. This is not about attachment or getting back with a past love.

You are the sun and the core of it exists in these tiny pockets of memory in your heart. The sunshine of love comes from you and it is the total of love that you have for everyone you know, and have ever known. Every one of those people has a pocket in your heart. This is the source of so much inner-wealth. We must not wait to be loved to be in love. Love does not come to us it comes from us. We cannot be loved more than we love. So when we are in suffering it's because we have stopped loving one or two of those love pockets. When we stop sending out sunshine, when we stop honouring the true source of love, the pockets that exist in our heart. Learn to love one of them, learn to love thousands. There is an unlimited supply.

Keeping the love pockets open and the sun shining in your life.

Love comes from you, not to you. So it's important to keep the love pockets in your heart glowing. Try taking time to sit quietly in nature daily and imagine how much you love your lover, or ex-lover: just drop any expectation of them. Consider all the issues you see in them as a mirror of you. By finding the balance, see if you can love those issues in you. You must remain committed to continuously improving this skill of discernment between a love free of expectation and a love filled with judgments and projection. The real power you have in life is to drop your ego driven judgments of right and wrong. Just love. Hold the love for people you know and have known as the most important ingredient for your ability to love yourself and your partner. This is nature's healing.

Daily ritual.

We bring our devotion into everyday life through the art of ritual. Rituals are more than acts of anchoring; they become acts of devotion to something beyond the self.

Ritual is an act of respect for someone or something outside us, a large or small act of giving without need or desire to receive. Ritual can be spontaneous, but the true value of ritual is a relentless commitment, come rain, hail or shine.

That is the difference between doing something for ego, and doing it for ritual. Steadiness is the mark of ritual. Rituals of steadiness are repeated day, after day, after day. They are not for self, but are a mark of respect for something higher, like a purpose in life.

Ritual is how we bridge the inspiration of our inner stillness with the spontaneity of everyday life. If you walk around India, you will see this ritual as a way of life. Small paintings on doorsteps, the day couldn't begin without them, or the candles lit in the hall in honour of a deceased relative, or incense burning as a thank you to the Gods. Flowers adorn alters, not requesting privilege, but as an act of ritual. And nothing could prevent it happening. It is a mark of respect to something bigger than the individual.

Rituals are acts of devotion. Here are some wonderful examples that people have developed and shared with me over the years. Remember, ritual is not an act of manifestation of anything; it is a remembrance of the divine nature of life.

- Maintaining an altar in your home and keeping it clean daily.
- Lighting a candle in the evening.
- Saying a prayer of thank you at mealtime.
- Holding hands in the park.
- Maintaining a garden.
- Having a photo wall of those you love.
- Having an affirmation wall with pictures of future dreams on it.
- Writing love letters to each other and posting them.
- Cleaning the kitchen as an act of love.
- Saving money according to an agreed plan for the future.
- Never going to bed with an argument in progress.
- Loyalty, always standing up for and speaking well of your lover.
- Prioritisation of your relationship over other things.
- Maintaining health and wellness so you can turn up for love.

Can you see that we can re arrange many everyday tasks so they become acts of love? Even taking the garbage out can become a ritual act of love that makes your partners life easier. Then we are acting with loving intent and it will be rewarded ten fold. In this way we are not feeding the ego through what we do, but are humble to ritual. The key is to be willing to maintain that ritual even when you don't want to, or need to, any longer. These are just a few ideas on the rituals of love. I am sure you can think of a few more unique ones between you. Remember to make them every day events and easy.

"Today, love without expectation. Love someone you hate, love someone you fear, love someone you left behind and don't take his or her reaction to heart. Make every day a Valentines Day, and see how many people you can honour, past present and future. Love them from a place if gratefulness. Love them knowing tomorrow may never come and know that the deepest regret any human being can have, is to hold back their love, even for a second."

"Today, light a candle in your heart for all those people that you love or have loved. Drink a glass of fresh water to their beauty, their gifts and their ways. Hope and wish that today, on this everyday Valentines Day, they are in love, with love and they are happy. What else could real love be, but the wish for someone else's happiness?"

"Loving acts are acts done out of love, because of love, and without the expectation of love in return."

Stay humble – Small acts keep your heart open.

Humility is important as well. To get past the Ego is to cut away the rough edges of vanity, which hurts and disturbs those one meets in life. Vanity is separateness. Truly loving individuals will recognise themselves in others, and rather than judge them as less, they appreciate the mirror. It is of no service to yourself or your relationship to judge another as less or more. It is expansive to acknowledge our own humility. So many of life's stresses can be extinguished at the source if we are able to recognise ourselves in others.

Devotion means that our lover's happiness becomes a high priority.

This is the demonstration of our love. There is nothing more important, nothing more potent, than the small acts of our devotion. We dedicate every circumstance we can to their improvement and happiness.

Opening your heart pockets when they are jammed – some ideas.

Contemplate the meanings of the revealed books of the sacred traditions, and the words of the saints, since these perform an action upon the heart, removing its illusions, healing its ills, restoring its strength.

The same function can be served by inspired art, literature, and music, which also perform an action upon us. Another cure for the heart is keeping one's stomach empty. Any excess of food hardens the heart.

Fasting is the opposite of the subtle and not so subtle addictions with which we numb ourselves to the experience of heart. When through fasting we expose the heart's pain to ourselves, we become more emotionally vulnerable and honest. And then, can the heart be healed.

Prayer before sunrise is a powerful inspiration. In these early morning hours the activity of the world has been reduced to its minimum, the psychic atmosphere has become still, and we are more able to reach the depths of concentration upon our own conscious.

Finally, keeping company with "heart" people can restore faith and health to the heart.

It is only a matter of degree to move from the ailing heart to the purified heart.

Centre yourself and all your attention in the reality of divine love, which has the power to unify our fragmented being and reconnect us with unity at all levels of existence.

Minimising your psychological distortions by over coming the slavery of your attractions, and seeing beyond the veil of selfishness.

Then, in that state, we may discover a deep receptivity a spiritual presence within. When we can centre ourselves and our attentions on the presence of divine reality, we not only become unified within ourselves, we recognise our unity with all of life. This is the unifying function of the heart. Knowing Love.

Rumi on Love.

"All desires, affections, loves, and fondness's people have for all sorts of things, such as fathers, mothers, friends, the heavens and the earth, gardens, pavilions, works, knowledge food, and drink - one should realise that every desire is a desire for love, and other things are just 'veils'. When one passes beyond this world and sees the 'coverings' and that what they were seeking was in reality one thing. All problems will then be solved. All the heart's questions and difficulties will be answered, and everything will become clear. God's reply is not such that he must answer each and every problem individually. With just one answer all problems are solved."

To be inspired in love, surrender to it.

To stay in Love means we come down into the dirty, ordinary, street scene of reality. That is where real devotion and love exists. When we love someone we must learn to trust ourselves, surrender to love. This does not involve preparing for a soft landing, being half in and half out, hedging your bets. Nobody ever succeeded by creating escape routes. It means keeping the love pocket open to that person no matter what they do.

To keep the love pockets open you need to surrender to love. Today, and every day, fall in love, again, and again and again. Give more than is expected of you. Expect no reward. The beauty of love will be half won when you learn the secret of putting out more than is expected in all that you do. Make yourself so valuable to your beloved that eventually you will become indispensable. Find their dream and help them live it. Exercise your privilege to support their journey, go the extra mile, and enjoy all the rewards you receive. You deserve them!

"Today

Do something special for someone out of love.
Laugh even if you have to invent it
Cry one tear of gratitude
Accept a gift
Live a dream
Use Magic
Float
Stay still for just 5 minutes on your own
Breath a breath of life giving air
Clear your mind for 30 seconds
Look up
Say thank you
Give somebody a special treat
Be Gentle
Step back from it all for just one long breath.
Succeed."

To keep your heart pockets open, and to stay in love, is to surrender to another person. Then we open to direct communication. There is no trust required if the ego is soft. To be in a relationship, and celebrate the spontaneity of falling in love, we cannot hide. We cannot be embarrassed about our strange collection of qualities. We present everything as it is. And in return we must welcome our lover, without ego, and accept their strange collection of qualities too. Surrender means working together with love. You cannot take the moral high ground and still hold love sacred. You cannot surrender to love and then say, "If".

Surrender means, "Here I am, and here you are". There is no need to make you better so that "I can love you in the future". There is no "if" in love.

To surrender means you'll need to get used to marching directly into disappointment, work with disappointment, go into it, and make it an acceptable and important part of your way of life. Your expectations are not true, they are the barriers to the journey of love, so you must stop hoping to achieve them in your relationship, not want to achieve them, but to dismantle them.

Disappointment is a good sign of loving intelligence, because it reveals honesty between your expectations and your love. It cannot be compared to anything else; it is so sharp, precise, obvious and direct. If we can open, surrender to love then we suddenly see that our expectations are not going to be met, no matter how much we try. Every time we try to change somebody, move them or shift them, love dies. Wanting things to be different than they are is the mark of the ego. This is not love, this is the ego. They are opposites. So it takes courage to say, "You didn't meet my expectations, and that revealed how much I needed to grow." This is sacred love. A moving soft ego always looking to adapt.

Love actually means being prepared to land on hard, ordinary ground, on the rocky, wild countryside of confrontation of your own issues. What you don't like in your lover is a mirror of your ego. Once we open ourselves, then we land on what is, it's disappointing, and this is the real beauty of love. People can reject your expectations; they cannot reject your love.

In true love, you have to allow your "mind and body" to surrender, it means adapt, remain flexible. There is nothing to fear losing once you identify with the simplicity of surrender. The only thing that can be hurt is your ego, so if you can develop a soft ego, you will be free to hold that power of love anytime you choose. If your ego can flex, then there is no hurt. Instead of taking the ego and emotions so seriously, take love seriously. Love can shine through everything. The key to doing this is to surrender the moral high ground, and automatically you soften your ego, you.

It is easy to love when you first "fall in love", because your mind was out of the way and your heart was free to love but then your mind remembers the past, or projects its expectations out for the future and all that unhealed baggage starts to subconsciously surface. Everyday relationship starts to bring memories and expectations back. Inch by inch our heart can get blocked by all the unfinished business from the past.

I went out with a lady who, many years before, had a teenage love affair. She was so badly affected by the loss of it that her chest collapsed. From then on, all her partners were older men because she thought they would not "dump her" like that boy in her teens.

She found that she could love for the first weeks of a new affair, but after that, she was crazy in fear, hyper sensitive to all her issues. You could say she was very messed up, but really it was a blockage in her heart to that one boy so long ago, and it had never been fixed. What was amazing for me to observe was that the more I gave her love, the more her issues surfaced. My love pushed her back into her issues. Her consciousness was stuck in her past. We know that we can't be a prophet in our own home; so, there was nothing I could do to help. I just loved her and let nature bring her what was necessary.

Don't hold back.

Now this is of vital importance if you truly want to keep your heart pockets open and fall in love again. The person who is holding back love for one person in the past cannot fully release it to another because they are closed, afraid of that suffering. So they remain broken hearted but try to get on with their lives. This just doesn't work because the past haunts them and keeps those love pockets shut. Remember, love comes from us, not to us.

Our blocked love pockets are also contagious. What we judge in the past (unhealed or forgiven) we breed in our children, attract in a partner, or become. So the past always haunts us. If you can't love the past then you are simply running away from it but carrying all the baggage.

So, to heal – really heal the past - there are two important issues. One is to love the person who hurt you. You loved them before, so you can love them now. And the second issue is to deal with the pain or shattered expectation (emotions) and that part is really simple. Just know that the laws of nature (your real connection to God) reveal that there are two sides to everything. So there can't be a bad thing without good in it. That's universal love. Support and challenge all in the same package.

"Whatever your situation in life, love must feature in the formation of your world. This love should be as fresh, free, and as far-reaching as the morning breeze. It must be warmed by the sunshine so that your life can be warmed by the celebration of love."

The irony (Dante calls it the cosmic giggle) is that the person who hurt you most is no doubt the person you loved most. So the greatest suffering, and the greatest pain, are often in the one circumstance. Your ego will explain a thousand reasons why you shouldn't love them. But you do. Once you love someone you can't retract it. You love them forever no matter how naughty they were.

They live in tiny love pockets within your heart. There are thousands of these pockets, you accumulate these loves, even if they leave, die, hurt you or just pass you in the street. Little pockets in your heart for those you loved and love; and they must be healthy.

Chapter 10. Personal Harmony
Do What You Love & Love What You Do

In this chapter we discuss the power of doing what you love and the essential keys to sustaining it.

To have an inspired day, don't clutter your hours with so much "business" and unimportant things that you have no time to "be in love" and "live with love". This applies to play as well as work. A day merely survived, with money as the only reward, is no cause for celebration. In its purified state, the human heart is the hologram of the seen and unseen worlds; it is the part that reflects the whole. The heart is the point at which the individual human being is closest to the Divine. The heart is the centre of our motivation and our knowing, possessing a depth and strength of will that the personality lacks. When we say that the heart has an integrative power, we are not talking in abstract, metaphorical, or merely intellectual terms. The realisation and purification of the heart both opens a doorway to the infinite and results in a restructuring of neural pathways - a refinement and reorganisation of our entire nervous system - that allows the fullest expression of our human possibilities. We can so easily fall into the world of live to work rather than work to live. Time can rush by; we are so busy getting ready to enjoy life that we are too tired to take advantage of it. To manage our life for the benefit of love we must master the power of will. This, in another language, means discipline.

Bringing it home.

Work with love, live with love, act with love, a home with love, friendships with love, heal with love. Love is a lifestyle. Love is not separate from our life because actually, love is life. We grow with love and stay young with love. Our health thrives on it; our joy is underpinned by it. A person who loves their work is unstoppable, inspired. It all begins at home. A sanctuary of love. This is a chaotic home, a place where feelings and experiences are honest, and challenges are many. But there is always a smile; we call it the mystical smile, because you know that all the challenge is not in conflict with love. It is simply your ego, trying to protect itself. Like an angry child. The key to living with love is the ability to fall through that ego, to the truth that sits beneath it, any time you choose. This is the mark of wisdom.

To maintain your inspiration start by doing what you love and loving what you do. Just for arguments sake let's block out your vision of the world so you can't see your daily life any more. There's nothing there.

You are sitting here reading this great article then no matter who is around you, you are alone. Now, imagine. There are about 6 trillion stars in the Milky Way. Our Sun is one of them. And our planet goes around our Sun, just like all the other Suns have planets too. There are 50 billion galaxies like the Milky Way. So, if you do the math, your calculator will be unable to display the numbers because we aren't normally built to think that big.

Now the world is still painted out in everyday terms but sitting alone you find yourself in awe of another dimension. This is the most important thing. To stay in awe of the magnificence of the universe and how totally lucky we are to be conscious of the vast magnificence of it. To stay inspired we have to get over the tenancy to make our current reality the only universe we know because that makes us self obsessed: de-motivated.

To have a really, really inspired day, one of the greatest gifts is simply to be excited about the fact that you're alive. The gift is just knowing that you are alive and have the opportunity to see stars and moons and beauty in a flower. My Dad used to say, "I look up the obituaries in the paper, if I'm not in it; then it's a great day".

We each need to remain so excited about life, just like a child at Christmas or Passover or whatever your faith's special day. Everyday is Christmas; everyday is your birthday, the birth of a new day. That's where great, fantastic, unbelievable days begin.

In your home, surround yourself with things from another world. Not this one. Pictures of a universe, like my screen saver from Apple. Amazing awe-inspiring ideas and things that make you like a child so ready to have a fantastic day. Like a child learn to bounce off the walls and mend the hits. Make no excuses and be like a child, smile, want life, want it to be fun. In this, you will know yourself and your heart will be open to life.

Create with love.

To manifest anything without inspiration or love is totally possible. But never enjoyable. To manifest a child on this earth without love is not enjoyable, it is a task. To manifest a business without inspiration becomes a job, not a passion of love. To do anything without love as your centre is to manifest with force and emotion and there can be no rest in this heart.

So inspiration and love for what you do is the centre, and its purpose is to expand. Love expands by the act of doing things, by creating homes, building families, expanding businesses, imagining new songs. Manifest is the result of love. All of life is about creating and when we create with love, we are living on purpose.

Love and inspiration need maintenance. We may begin to manifest a relationship with love but the challenges can overcome the love. We might begin with love, but emotions and judgments creep in. Then we are motivated to start doing things in our relationship to try to overcome the lack of love. People start making babies, growing children, building homes, collecting friends, because they've 'got to' compensate for diminishing love, trying to make their relationship work. They substitute material things for the love that was meant to be behind their life. Then, there is manifestation without love. The love was there, but the problems and challenges have overcome the love.

The four substitutes for real inspired love in life are; Spirituality – trying to get what we've already got. Food and substance - which fills the vacuum that is meant for love. Sexuality - the physical, emotional and sexual escape from real intimacy. Greed - the mindless accumulation of property, assets and personal goods in an attempt to feel good about being uninspired.

The standard solution to lost inspiration in life is to increase the emphasis on substitutes. People start wanting more sex, more money, more work, and more "uppers". They keep the same old process of dealing with their challenges and just look for another place to get fulfilled, down in the lower mind. But this doesn't last because that person always gets ill. It's the cause of many of the diseases people get - patched over lost love using substitutes. There is a better way.

Instead of substitutes and putting band-aids on issues, it is better to go to the source and actually find what is stopping a person from doing what is the most important and most natural thing on earth for them, loving what they do.

Everyday there are challenges in your life. Everyday there is an opportunity to grow in love.

Then there is growth. By wanting to stay inspired everyday leads you to a process of growing your love through issues. That process is revealed in nature. Without human interference, the laws of nature reveal the universal beauty of love, and therefore any issue you pass through their guidance will turn, from an ego emotion, to love. This is the how we return to our true nature; ask the nature from whence we came, to guide us.

Inspiration in action.

Discipline is the turning point. The pain of regret always outweighs the pain of discipline. Therefore, as we shift from the ego focus of short term pleasure toward purpose, dreams and longer term results, the ego loses control and becomes the lion, and you to tamer, The vast majority of spiritual practices like yoga, meditation, tai chi and more hold this as the most critical ingredient of the transformation between ego life and love life. Discipline.

Will is a different kind of power. Will acknowledges that there are temptations, that there are always old patterns, but that all the righteousness, devotion and fanatic adherence to dogma will never remove the source of temptation. An alcoholic is still an alcoholic while they are in a phobia about alcohol. With will power there is a different approach; there is simply something more important to do.

Will does not rely on righteousness or goods that are separated from bad. Like the healing fanatic who will tell you about the virtues of organic food **for hours on end**. No, that is the ego in blind fanaticism building dogma, separation. There are two sides to everything, good and bad, including organic food. But will is different. Will asks, "What are my long term goals and what choices are best for me to make to achieve them?" Like, "I want to travel the world helping children". I would ask "When?" and you might say, "Until the day I die", and I might say "When?" and you might add, "OK, when I am 90". So now we got past a loose fantasy with no detail, to a little more detail. Then we go for lunch and you are sitting opposite me and when menu comes I ask, "What are you having for lunch?" You think, and say, "Oh there are so many delicious choices", and I would reply, "Not if you are serious about living until you are 90 and still travelling around the world helping children." Then you might choose the organic salad, because it might help you live your dream. That choice is made with 'will power'.

Doing what you love – wise choices.

How are we going to choose? There are always at least two alternatives. Emotional choices and love choices. They are like two carrots dangled in front of our nose almost constantly; one goes left, the other goes right. Emotion will make us happy and give short- term gratification. Love may not be as stimulating, but in the long-term pays truth. So, will power is the power to make that choice. Given that an inspired life is a doing life, these choices are crucial.

If you want to be a rock guitarist, then you'd better have will power. Because you'll need to practice everyday, even when your emotions are all over the ship. Every day you might feel tired or depressed, or happy and joyful and, if like the average person, you follow those emotions, like an undisciplined child. Then 10 years later you'll be so expert in being emotional, but not one day closer to playing the guitar.

That's the average relationship. Dreaming of sacred love, wanting to grow into the future together, committed to all sorts of wonderful destiny, but just acting on emotion. If there is no will power then there is no God power, no love power. If you can't apply discipline to your relationship how are you going to go anywhere but around in circles? Will power means to process judgement, to give each other priority. It means don't sweat the small stuff, forget being right, stop giving advice when it is not asked for, learn how to love instead of change things. This is love power. Real discipline.

If you say you are going to do something in your life, and you don't do it, you beat yourself up. Make commitments of discipline in your relationship. If you break them, don't lie. Admit it. No one can beat you up more than you. But then work on more discipline, more will, more love power by finding a better reason to follow your commitment. Being committed to something is all about having a good enough reason. If you love yourself enough then emotional blackmail is not a good enough reason to be committed. If someone says, "I won't like you if you don't do that" then only if you already hate yourself is that a motive. But at this level of will there has to be a dream you'd love so much that the cost of emotion is too high and not worth the worry.

People get this when they lose something. I had a friend who had a heart attack. They were so not disciplined and had absolutely no will power. After that catastrophe they became a health fanatic. A year later they were emotional again and eating junk. They were disciplined out of fear. This is not sustainable. In your relationship, find a dream that is big enough that you would love to live and then work out what the cost is in terms of lifestyle. If you aren't willing to pay the price get out of the way so someone else can live it. But don't expect your relationship to last if you can't find a dream worth living for.

After two or three shattered dreams you might find it hard to come up with real commitments for long-term dreams. Simply start with little ones and work your way up. There is a process in the last chapters of this book on dream matching.

The will of the human heart is an unbridled experience of doing something that you love, rather than something that loves you. Then you bring this choice making awareness into all facets of your life without compromise. Will is the heart choosing long-term benefit over short-term emotional expression.

Inspiration is not found in emotional drama but in the wisdom of choices and sacrifices made in recognition of dreams and Love. If you do not have the will to choose wisely then you'll pick low priority activities to fill your mind. Because these are self sabotaging (they do not fulfil your dreams), your lover won't be able to wait for you to grow up in love and will probably leave you. If you are treating yourself as unworthy of love, unworthy of higher purpose, unworthy of long-term investment, then your lover will not treat you any differently. Remember that nobody does to you more than you do to yourself. Will is love; will power is self-love.

Self-love is found in the doing of life, not in the thinking of it. Self-love is action of choices. Your self worth grows when you do things worthy of your own respect. Emotional drama and working on low priorities, working on other people's priorities, living vicariously through children, is all self-deception. Nature will not have it. Nature will bring disaster, catastrophe and humbling circumstances to anyone who does not work on the higher priorities that manifest their dreams. If you do not have a dream, there is only ego to love.

A person who can say, “I love doing this” is far more rewarded on the cosmic level than the ego that would profess, “I love this, because these are the things I get for doing it”. Achievements last for moments, but life is a journey. There is no solace for the wealthy person who, surrounded with material items and victories, cannot smile in the face of a days work, or at the idea of walking to the garden for a few moments of reflection. It is in the eyes of loved ones where we find God rather than the buildings we create to house them. It is in the doing of things of high priority to our dreams that the wealth exists, not in the gratitude of those we help.

Will is not power, although it is all the power that exists. How does creation function in the universe? The world? The answer is, by Will. The laws of the universe hold all the chaos into a magnificent order. The entire universe conforms to just five simple laws. Therefore, what we call our willpower is more accurately, God power; and emotion is hell power. Will power is a combination of physical and mental strength. Our hands, with all their perfect mechanics, cannot hold a glass of water if there is no willpower to support it. If will power fails us, a seemingly healthy person will not be able to even stand. Therefore, fish do not swim with their body; they swim with their will power. And when man has the will to swim, he swims like fish.

Will power has enabled humankind to complete tremendous things. Will brings us to success, yet when will fails, however intelligent the person, they too fail. Therefore, it is not the human power solely that moves us, it is a divine power found in the human body that makes unbelievable feats possible. The work of the mind is still greater, for no one can hold a thought in his or her mind for a moment if there is not the strength of will to hold it. If a person cannot concentrate and keep their thoughts still for a moment it means that will power fails them, as it is will that holds a thought.

Will power is love; in spiritual terms, love is will power. If one says, "God is love", it means in reality “God is Will”. The love of God, the Will of God, causes the creation, “Thy will be done on earth as it is in heaven”. Universal laws pervade our earth and our heaven. When a person says, “I love to do it”, it means, “I will to do it”, which is a stronger expression and means, “I fully love to do it with all my heart and soul.”

"Birth, water, fire, air seemed to us as things, as objects, but before God they are living beings; they stand as his obedient servant's and obey divine Will".

Rumi,

We received a part of that divine will as our own divine heritage, and it is our consciousness of that will which makes it greater. If we are not conscious of it, our will becomes smaller. An optimistic attitude towards life develops the power of will, while the pessimistic attitude reduces it. Thus, it is only ourselves that hinders our progress in life. There is no one in the world that can be a worse enemy than ourselves; for at every failure we see ourselves standing in our own light.

When the mind is pushed to hold one thought for a while it becomes restless because it is not accustomed to discipline. The mind by itself has no hesitation to hold a thought of disappointment, blame, anger, pain grief, sorrow or failure; it will hold it so tightly that you cannot take one of those righteous thoughts from its grip. But when the mind is requested to hold a particular affirmative thought, often it will not, responding instead by saying, "I am free and I will not be controlled". This is the ego fighting against the heart of will for emotional freedom and cursing the divinity of sacred love, dreams and joy.

You must teach your mind discipline by concentration; power of will, then the mind becomes tied in concentration to the focus of your work. A parent must be strong with a child because they have no discipline. They must be that higher wisdom until the child becomes wise. A disciplined mind becomes your servant rather than your master. The thoughts of the heart, and the act of holding the thought in the heart, are both of great importance for the fulfilment of an individual's life, and most importantly, their relationships.

Often a person will say, "I try my best but I cannot get my mind to concentrate, I cannot make my mind still". While it is true they cannot concentrate, it's not true that they try their best. Once the mind has become your servant, what more can you wish? Then your world is your own, you are the king or queen of your kingdom. Although some people will argue, "Why not let the mind be free, as we are free?" But the easy answer to this is to observe the life of the person without discipline, filled with emotional drama, maybe even a filled bank balance. They have lost the essence; they are nothing but living shells of emotion.

Self-discipline is that which makes the master of the self, however difficult and tyrannical it may seem in the beginning. Self-mastery is a combination of discipline and applied will. It is not in vain that the great sages live in caves with devotion and great purpose. It is not something to imitate, but something to understand. Such asceticism is self-discipline; it is the development of will power. This is the turning point for a sacred relationship. To invest yourself in love is to have the will to sustain it.

There are those who would sit for the whole of their lives under the coconut tree and wait for the coconuts to drop. There are those who would chop the tree, so they own the tree. There are those who would learn to climb and bring what they need to their lives. Too many of us enter a relationship and then wait to see what happens. We buy the furniture and make the babies. There is no brain required in either of those actions and we can have pleasured sex with 90% of our brain removed. Love is will, effort, and without affirmative effort, you wait for the coconut, and survive on nothing between.

"The Tao, or Way, has never been put down in words; rather it is left for the seeker to discover within. Taoism is concerned with man's spiritual level of being, and in the Tao-Te-Ching the awakened man is compared to bamboo: upright, simple, useful outside and hollow inside. A uniquely Taoist concept is wu-wei, non-action. This does not mean "no action", but rather, not spontaneous action (reaction) that accords with needs as they naturally arise. If we keep still and listen to the inner promptings of the Tao, we shall act effortlessly, efficiently, hardly giving the matter a thought. We will be ourselves, as we are. The Tao is the natural way of all beings; it is the nameless beginning of heaven and earth. Yet it lies hidden, transmitting its power and perfection to all things. Only one who is free of desire can apprehend the Tao. There is no Personal God in Taoism, and thus no union with Him. There are three worlds and beings within them, and worship is part of the path. The Taoist observes wu-wei, or non-doing, like water that without effort seeks and finds its proper level. This path includes purifying oneself through stilling the appetites and the emotions; accomplished in part through meditation, breath control and other forms of inner discipline... The foremost practice is goodness or naturalness, and detachment from the Ten Thousand Things of the world."

Chapter 11. Everyone Dies but Not Everyone Lives Living Your Vision

"When you are inspired by some greater purpose, some extraordinary project, all your thoughts break their bonds, your mind transcends limitations, your consciousness expands in every direction, and you find yourself in a new, great, and wonderful world. Dormant forces, faculties and talents become alive and you discover yourself to be a greater person by far than you ever dreamed yourself to be."

Pattanjali

In this chapter we ask deeper questions like: Why were we born? What purpose could there be that is higher than ourselves? These are great questions of all inspired people.

Native American and First Nation people have their own versions of Vision Quests; this process I am about to describe is not the same as theirs. It is important to say that because it is easy to use the term "Vision Quest" and have people think I am talking about a Native Tradition. No, this is not correct, I am not talking about any cultural tradition, I am talking about you, your heart, your soul, your true nature, tapping it, and then finding the inspiration that exists in your heart. The process I describe belongs to no one, it is a part of nature.

The real source of a vision quest are four questions planted inside the human psyche, and they remain the real search of all humanity. The places people look for answers are very strange sometimes, but the search is the same. The one who leads the mass of humanity has the most certainty of the answers. Self-made people who don't want to follow organised religions or groups go looking for their own answers.

1. Who am I? (In other words - what is my role in life?)
2. Where am I going? (In other words what is the future)
3. Where have I been? (In other words how did I get here?)
4. Why am I here? (In other words what is the meaning of this life?)

The person with the greatest certainty of these four questions leads. In kindergarten it just might be the kindergarten teacher. You came from home, you are going home, you are here to play and you are a wonderful child. Of course, as we grow, so does the need for bigger answers.

It could even end up – where was I before I was born, where am I going after I die? What am I here on earth to do? And the last, who am I really, because I know I am not who I thought I was?

There are no half hearted success stories.

We speak of the heart as if it were a spongy weak mushy place that opens at movies, dribbles that tear down your cheek at the worst of moments, and makes us so vulnerable. And so it might be. But the heart is without doubt the most powerful human centre that can exist. All humanitarian power comes from the human heart - all compassion, motivation, consideration and inspired leadership. This is the experience we have in the presence of a powerful individual, a leader, performer or lover. An open heart is the greatest power any human can contain within their body. It is the true meeting place of heaven and earth. The symbol of the crucifixion, a vertical line reaching to heaven, the vertical line below going to earth, and our arms outstretched – good and evil.

The heart is the centre where all these points meet. All the teachings of the great masters who have walked this earth are centred in the heart. This is not, as many people think, acting with love. It is acting with will and the greatest will a human can hold exists in the heart.

When you put two electrical leads together they spark as power surges through the wires; the sparks are hot, on fire, they are the heart. This is the junction of the highest power of love, meeting the highest power of the ego. The spark is huge. This is will. The ego tamed and focused on a purpose bigger than itself; the love channels open to higher power. They meet in this centre and there is the greatest power known to humanity.

If the heart goes out of something, the individual goes out. We sabotage anything that we cannot link to our purpose. This is the heart at work, subconsciously or consciously guiding us through life.

Doing your own vision quest.

"Give me a few hours by myself, let me alone, shut out all interruptions, and I can bring myself down to my work. I take my pen in hand. I write a few thoughts. I see the future. And realise my responsibility. The more I think of the duty placed on me, the graver since my responsibility. Every idea has weight. I can see the effect of days ahead."

I had heard of a place in Nepal where there are sacred lakes. After I came back from that feeble attempt to become another Snow Leopard legend, I turned my sights to those lakes. I trekked for 15 days through villages, high into the mountains on well-worn paths to reach them. And it was here, sitting on the slopes surrounding those lakes, that I learned how to undertake a vision quest. My first.

When I went to those sacred lakes, I spoke to the clouds, and they spoke to the clouds that covered my heart. I spoke to the mountains and they revealed the mighty truth that lay hidden within. I spoke to the sacred lake and it reflected beauty back to me, reminding me to do what I do with love. I called to the spirits of these mountains, and they took my hand and showed me the path. And there on that slope, in the hot sun, the cold wind, surrounded by the love of these Sacred Mountains on top of the world, I got my dream renewed.

Every year I take small groups of people to these sacred lakes. They go to find a deeper essence of life, to renew their individual commitment to authenticity. People sit by those lakes and dream, and there is no ego involved. Ego falls off on the way up. These lakes are a place where, legend has it, the power of prayers are multiplied by thousands upon thousands, a place where dreams that are dreamed, come true. And for me that has always been the case.

Here are a few tips:

1. Don't be afraid. There is a wisdom far greater than the one you know as your mind. Let the dreams come, let them fly on the wings of love, and let them sit. Allow them a home, a resting place, because those dreams have been waiting for you to arrive. Let them find you, that is enough.

2. Hold those dreams sacred; share them with your beloved. Allow no soul to condemn, question, advise, interfere, compromise or criticise them. Prevent yourself from judging, or having the mindset to ask how, or why. Those two words kill the spirit of a dream.

3. Practice dreaming without action. I would like to share an example. You have a mother. Look up from where you are seated now, and see around you one thing that reminds you of her. Then come back to this page and read on. Did you think, "What should I find?" Did you ask, "What sort of object?" Did you immediately find something, but it didn't seem right so you rejected it? This is the ego. That is why vision quests need to be learned. Eventually you will learn to hold your mind empty and allow your intuition to make choices without good reason.

4. Don't dream about how you want to feel, who you want to become, how you want to change yourself. All this comes from judgment, and that judgment is from your mind. Dream only of doing. What would I love to do? This is the only area where spirit can guide you. Who you are, and who you become is irrelevant to a vision quest. Only your ego cares about that.

5. Always ask. Don't force the answer. Don't judge the result. Be thankful for the opportunity you have to hear. Avoid wanting anything. Ambivalence is the state of mind in which inspiration will come to you. Just be open.

6. Remove all your hopes. Most blockages in visioning come from wanting. Wanting to be peaceful, wanting to be loving, wanting to be nice, wanting to be spiritual. Wanting is blockage. True visioning means, "Whatever it takes, I will follow the guidance I get."

7. Don't be bluffed by others. These days, self-help language is freely available, gurus abound, spiritual teachers are many and bookshops are filled with anything from how to hurt people (turn your boyfriend into a frog) to how to call down an angel. It is hard to know people now, because we have so much language. People can talk the talk, but can they walk the walk? Walk the talk. If you want to really know a person, see what they do, and how they do it. All else is myth.

Don't BS yourself in creating your vision. It must be pure.

The higher you get in life, the more important it is to eliminate puffery from your vision. There's more at stake and your power of influence extends to many people. However, all people no matter what their age must be wise in the science of removing their ego from vision setting.

Sometimes we use the future to get out of the present, but if we use the future as a fantasy, that future never comes and the present gets worse. I advise my clients never to go on holiday to "someday I'll" (someday Isle) that's a place in the future that usually never comes. The other place I advise my clients to avoid is "when-I". 'When I' defers current happiness and refers it to a place in the future. It means that life can be crappy right now because it's worth it for some future result. Sadly, the crappy life is really a mindset, and it travels into the future to destroy happiness there too.

There is a vast difference between a vision and a fantasy. The primary difference being that fantasies paint the future without disasters and challenges. They can only come true in half. Visions are not emotional, fantasies are nothing but. A fantasy might be an aspiration for an all upside existence; a successful career, a happy family, a wonderful relationship, a family holiday. They are oxymorons. One sided fantasies that have no pain. They are most common in people with depression. It is a hope for an all upside experience. And therefore those visions never manifest as they were expected.

I worked with 55 youths at risk in Canada in an Indigenous community. They were amazing, probably more genius than anything else. Normality bored them. Some were on Ritalin yet they had amazing gifts. There was a temptation to inspire these youth by creating visions of the future that were aspiring.

However, just that issue caused their suicidal tendencies. Depression and self-sabotage come because the real world doesn't match the fantasy world people have in their mind. Their lower mind creates a "smooth" path to achievement, filled with success and support. So the first sign of disaster, they slump into hell.

Over twenty years I have done thousands of business consultations with entrepreneurs. The hardest part of these consultations is to pull their business plans to bits. No entrepreneur even came to me when things were going fantastic. They are usually looking for a radical change in their business and personal fortunes and the business plan is the formula for it. But just like the vision statement I wrote at that seminar, there's often a conflict between 'hope' and 'reality.' As a personal and business advisor, sadly my focus must be on reality. In those consults sometimes it feels like I deflate people's balloons, like a kid at a fair whose balloon pops. I feel like a total heel, but chasing a fantasy is a terrible construct for life so separating fantasy from reality is part of the work.

"The professor from Harvard was on holiday in Mexico, he stood at his hotel window looking out over the ocean and each day he noticed a fisherman, That fisherman left the shored in his little boat each morning at 5.00am and returned at 7.00am. He unloaded his fish, took a breakfast and was finished his day's work by 10.00am. Then he sat beneath the coconut tree and enjoyed the rest of the day in bliss. The Harvard professor approached the fisherman and suggested that with three boats he could employ others and make more money. The fisherman borrowed money and eventually had three boats going out each day. Then the professor suggested that with a fleet of boats the fisherman would really be well off, in fact they could list on the stock exchange. They did so, and the professor then suggested that if they can raise their share price, the fisherman would be rich enough to go down to Mexico, find himself a little boat, he could go out every morning at any time he chose and come back, have his breakfast and then sit under a coconut tree for the rest of the day in bliss."

Your Vision must be driven by clear intent. They are not infatuations. So a Real Vision has a high focus on the why. When the why is big enough the how takes care of itself. “I will give all I can to help people”, “I will work diligently to create a conscious home”, “I choose love over emotion.” “I will build an orphanage in Nepal.” or “I will contribute to the world.”

Why do you want to live your vision? Why is it important to others? Why would people help you? Why is there a benefit to the world? Why is this important to you? Answer these questions first.

Get past fantasies.

I went to a seminar once to create an inspired vision. It was awesome. I came out with it all written down. How many millions I would make; how many orphans I would save; how many children I’d sire even though I’d had a vasectomy. I felt fantastic, and the speaker had earned their money. They said, "Write it down, and focus on it, and then it'll all come true" They missed the bit about a little bit of luck and reality creeping in.

Can you see support and challenge in every vision in your life?

Can you see equal good and bad in every significant person in your vision?

Can you see how circumstances of the past helped as well as hurt you equally?

Can you see two sides of both support and challenge in your vision?

Of all those above, is there anything that can happen to you that you are not thankful for?

"We speak of life purpose. Actually there is nothing on earth that is not on your purpose. Your ultimate purpose is to learn love and everything you do will teach you that. Whether you are in hospital, permanently different, being challenged. You are on purpose if you can learn to love more from life. Develop an inward belief in the sacredness of the whole and that humanity can be in tune with this sacredness. That there is a universe of love, and our ego is yet to see it is the journey we are on, with purpose. Place your mind on truthfulness and use purification to remove the "dust" which conceals our inherently divine nature and thus receive the blessings. Your spirit is a holy power living in the real world. All living things possess the Divine. This is being inspired. Observe all taboos; avoid things that cause toxin and pollution. Make your prayers and offerings to the temples of your life. Worship the Gods and Goddesses, in which you place your faith. The sacred fire is the symbol that fights evil, it is the great purifier and sustainer, and it is the nature of the sun itself. So keep a flame burning in your heart."

To live your life purpose, you will rise to a point where there is nothing to change in the world. You are no longer polarised by the idea of right and wrong, and instead see that every action, good or bad, results in a pro and a con. You will act because you love it. You might help the poor, not because it is right, but because you love doing that. You might make love to your partner, not because this is some obligation or because it is right or wrong, but because this is what you love to do. Love replaces right and wrong. There is a sense of completion, you are fulfilled, and no longer need to change anyone or yourself. Then you simply go about your life, giving and loving people because you find great joy in it. There is no need to tell anyone what you do because the ego is not important.

Live your own life.

To live your real life vision you must continually break the mould. I remember so clearly my father arguing with my brother, who had left school early to work as a sales clerk in a discount store, because he was about to quit his job. My father had grown up through the depression, and for him, this secure, safe, well-paid employment was as high as he thought my brother should aim.

Kim was not convinced. He left the job, went to college part time, worked his way through the advertising industry, and twenty years later has worked throughout the world, built and sold his own multi million dollar company, and is now chairman of one of the leading advertising companies in the world.

My sister was in the same predicament. She left school early, became a dental nurse, graduated from NIDA in Sydney (The National Institute of Dramatic Art Sydney Australia), then married and went to London where she studied law and became one of the worlds leading barristers. My father thought she was lucky getting that job as a dental nurse.

However, this story doesn't stop just because you overcome one circumstance and then outlive, exceed the expectations of your family roots. It continues until you die. We can so easily think "oh, I have achieved so much, I should be proud and find a good safe place from which to live my life" but nature will have none of it.

On one of my many weird and expensive adventures on the path of personal exploration, I decided to traverse a 30-day section of the Himalayas, in Nepal. A friend of mine was famous for her journeys into Tibet and Nepal, I idolised her achievements, and could see myself doing the same. You know the thoughts, "I can do that, and it looks really easy."

About four hours into this 30-day expedition, and after 6 months arduous preparation, I stopped in my tracks, sat down on my pack and began to cry. After months of training, thousands of dollars invested, getting all pumped up, promoting and chest thumping, I stopped, took off my pack and went into a tailspin. What the hell was I doing out here trying to be somebody else, living someone else's dream?

What became apparent was that I had outlived my own dreams. As a child in fairly humble circumstances, we dreamed of food on the table, a non-violent home, a good steady job and a loving family. It was now thirty years later and I had achieved all those dreams. I was lost, I was living other people's dreams because I had achieved all my own. That day comes to everyone.

Nature's purpose in life is to grow us and sometimes our belief is that we have grown enough. But we measure our growth badly. Growth in nature's language is the taking on of more responsibility. You can be absolutely sure, when a person you know is experiencing a catastrophe, disaster, or a humbling circumstance in their life, they have stopped growing. They have decided that peace and calm is more important than taking more responsibility. They have given up their dreams; they are listening to everyone outside of them telling them, like my loving father, that it's better to be safe than sorry.

Grow yourself – don't shrink.

Our conduct depends largely on our level of devotion to our vision because when we are dedicated to an inspired vision, we give of ourselves. Inspired vision centres us; it is a deep personal awareness. Sometimes people feel that whatever the work they are doing, it could not be sacred, not intended for them. They blame the work. The missing piece here is not what is wrong with the work they are doing, but rather understanding the work they are performing right now in the context of their life purpose. It is easy to blame our circumstances, but really it is our need to re-educate, re engineer our lives that is the issue.

Many people back off from life when nature is telling them to put their foot on the gas. The new age fortune-teller might say, "Oh, it's stressful, turn away" but they are mixed up, you shouldn't pay for that advice.

Stress is a gift. How else do we know when we've peaked and need new technologies for self-management? Human consciousness is an ever-evolving thing and stress shows where it's stuck. It's the radar. Incompetence is one of the important experiences of life because it shows where we need to grow, from order to chaos.

There are many options we have when we get stressed or overwhelmed or anxious. Most conventional ones involve backing off in some way. But you can be sure that all backing off process lead to cancer. Breast cancer, prostate cancer, lung cancer, money cancer, love cancer.

Nature doesn't listen to our complaints, so why should we? Nature says, "Evolve or die" this is really clear. It is the core inspiration of nature, evolve or die. So, stress shows that we are living in harmony with nature, we reached a peak and now need to learn new ways. Not to change what we do, but to do it differently. We must be prepared to grow, to challenge the box we put ourselves in.

Many people shy away from stress because it reveals a measure of their lack of consciousness. But being proud of a stress-free life is unconsciousness too. When people withdraw from the challenges and seek comfort or balance they are actually self-sabotaging their life. They get ill and old fast; they decay. In a relationship, if you want stress-free time, have an affair with someone who you don't live with. However, it doesn't last.

The same stress over and over is like a dog biting you 20 times as you go through the gate. The same stress year after year, hampering your life. I say "evolve-ya-bastard" it's not about avoiding the dog; it's about dealing with it so it doesn't bite. For example, if you don't find new ways to do the same job, you won't stay employed to do it because deep down you'll fear failure. You have to rise up, become smarter, then go back and do the old job, go through the same gate, without getting bitten (stressed).

So, stress is a real gift but only if you grow through it, evolve to a higher consciousness. In other words you do what stressed you before, without stress.

Let's pretend I speak for a living. I stand up in front of audiences; talk and I get paid for it. So, there's an expectation from the audience that it's going to be entertaining. My original self-imposed stress limit was 20 people. I can almost talk in front of that many and keep my underwear clean.

Now, as soon as I got comfortable with 20, strangely enough I get a booking for 40 people. Just the thought of it made me tremble. I could self-sabotage, which most people do, "Oh, I have a sore throat" or "Gee, I'm busy" or "There's a problem with those audiences, they make me nervous." Now, it's obvious that I can't face 40 people with the same headspace I had with 20. I'd be totally stuffed. To evolve, I seek help, and find a teacher or someone to show me the way to do it.

But if I did that 40 people talk with consciousness, guess what? I get a booking for 50. Damn, I thought it was over, I thought I was clever, but now I am dumb again. I have to go to a teacher again. But I can't go to that same teacher. He was perfect to get me from 20 to 40 but they're hopeless at 50 people audiences. Not only do I face new stress, I face new learning's, new teachers, and new teachings.

Coming back to the real world now, getting new teachers and learning new things all the time is a great treat because it can inspire me. However, as I am growing at 100 miles an hour, it is getting harder to find good teachers, not to mention very expensive. So, my suggestion is to learn something that grows with you.

The laws of nature are just such learning. They help you when you get a mosquito bite stress, and they help you when somebody dies. They help when you can't choose the brand of toothpaste or sell your billion-dollar property portfolio. The laws of nature don't answer questions, they teach you how to answer the questions yourself in a sustainable, inspired way. At each level of life they teach you how to deal with the stress.

Expanding your vision is a great antidote to stress too. When my vision is the size of an ant, then ants annoy me. When my vision is the size of my ego, all things in my ego annoy me. But if my vision is universal, wow, Pluto just went out of orbit. Small stuff just shoots by.

Face stress head on, change the way you deal with life not change your life. Keep your vision expansive; grow it as fast as you grow your love. They are one in the same.

How do we grow from stress?

1. Take whatever is bad and find good in it. There's order in the chaos.

2. See that nothing is missing just changes form. So the stress is already in your life in a different form and you dealt with it in another form quite well.

3. Stress can only exist at an ego level. Dig deeper within yourself and find your core. No stress there.

4. Worry about yourself causes stress. Worry about others causes no stress.

5. Deal with stress before it happens on three levels – Mind, body and Spirit. At the body level it is the nervous system that needs to evolve and yoga is one such process. At the mind level, the laws of nature put chaos into order, at the spirit level you find your inner peace, your core, your soul, try to preserve that connection at all times.

6. Remember that food, drugs, alcohol affect your nervous system.

7. Remember that the best answers exist when there's no emotion.

Chapter 12. Personal Healing
The Spirit of the Inner Child

One of the most influential healing experiences in my entire life was in counselling after my marriage break-up. I learned about my inner child, or in another language, my spirit. After 12 months getting to trust the process of counselling, my counsellor helped me find something quite amazing. There, underneath my macho facade, was a rejected child.

My mother died when I was three. She was here one moment, and gone the next. I was with her, just she and I, when we had an accident. She was thrown from the car and internally crushed. I sat beside her unconscious and bloodied body. Days later, I watched them lower her coffin into the ground. A strange stillness surrounded me, I could hear and see nothing; I could feel only love for her. I loved my mum, like any child does, and in that moment she was buried, it was all that I felt. I watched people crying, but couldn't understand why. I loved my mum.

In the years to follow I had to learn how to protect that innocence. My stepmother tried to beat me into submission, to love her. I couldn't understand why, because I did love her. But her definition of love was what I did, what I said, how I walked and talked. I couldn't understand because I loved my step mom.

I went to school and got beaten up from the first day to the last. My nickname was sunshine, but that sort of person doesn't fit easily into a school in the Australian Outback. I loved my schoolmates, but they didn't feel it. So, they beat me up, pushed my head under the water till I nearly drowned and created cruel tricks. I loved my friends, but they certainly didn't know it.

During the next 10 years on this journey with my step mom - who was by now a fully qualified alcoholic - and the confusion of being assaulted and victimised at school, I took matters into my own hands. I created a platform from which to fight back. A strong Chris.

I bought weight-training equipment and with the help of powder foods, built a powerful body. In two short years, at the age of 13, I turned street thug. I stole cars, broke into homes, carried knives and shared the streets with twelve of the worst and meanest people I have ever met, even to this day. By my 14th birthday, I was the only one who wasn't incarcerated or dead. So based on the overwhelming evidence that I was on the wrong track, I decided to fight the world in a different way. This time I built an ego out of success.

That ego lasted 20 years. In sport, business, community leadership, as a social activist, and university student I buried my love, that beautiful vulnerability beneath the structures and facade of my ego.

Eventually, my journey took me to Asia where I sat in Zen, staring at a wall. Nothing to say, nothing to do. If I lost concentration my perfectly upright posture would begin to sag. The monk would notice and I would be snapped, quite physically, and with shock, back to reality. Our eyes were open. There was no drifting off into fantasy worlds or other levels of the brain; reality, the wall, was enough.

When I left those retreats I could hear a pin drop, before it hit the ground. By staring at that wall we had learned to slice through emotion, past the desire to run away, past ambition, because there was nothing to be better at. We transcended the desire for the material, because what use is a million dollars while staring at a wall in a cabin in the forest? In effect, we learned to detach.

In these Zen retreats I would burst into tears for no reason, as if all the love that was so deeply buried would rise up, past the ego that I had grown to protect me but which had so little power in Zen meditation. It was a magical experience. It was just like sitting on the side of my mother's grave watching her coffin descend into those depths. This was love by the direct route, but how do you sustain it when you are back on the street, or in a business meeting with serious people?

So, now, jump ahead. Suddenly I'm in the middle of a divorce. And all this learning turns to crap. Everything gets stripped off and there's a child sitting by the graveside watching them lower his mother into the ground. Underneath all the façade including Yoga and Zen, there was an injured child.

Adults see things differently to kids. To everyone except me there were circumstances that were the cause of all the violence way beyond my little existence. But that's not how I saw it. Here I was: man, a millionaire, business owner, family man with three children, rowing champion, spiritual seeker and member of the school council, sitting in therapy dealing with a divorce, dribbling at the nose, acting like a three year old and trying desperately to stop himself from self destruction.

Over the next 12 months my therapist unwrapped the bandages from the thirty years of barrier building, one year, one event at a time. Back and back and back, until there, sitting in her room covered with a 34 year old body, sat a three year old child blaming himself for the death of his most precious love and attracting abuse he thought he deserved.

That boy, me, had encased himself in armour. Vulnerable and lonely I'd created masks and personalities, shelves full of trophies, bank accounts full of money, children, business and all sorts of other things to deny my existence, prove I was fine. But it was all a ruse. There in that counsellor's room held tight in safety, that three-year-old boy resurfaced. His name is "my spirit."

Like everyone else, there were things about my innocent child I always wanted to change. I resented that he was so soft. I was annoyed that he was clumsy and vulnerable. I was so embarrassed that he was so accident prone I blamed him for everything that went wrong, including humiliating me. It is a part of us all we want to keep secret and it's different for everyone. Ironically, I was later to find out that when doing advanced Zen, or sitting in a sweat lodge in Canada, this "secret" part of me was my greatest strength.

Ironically, I'd spend my whole life trying to hide him or at the least fix him. He was soft, gentle, and vulnerable and if anyone had asked what my flaws were, those would have been on the top of my list. In the march for self-development, I had tried to murder the most beautiful essence of my being.

Of course, most guys have this drama in some form or another. Sitting in the dust in my old outback home there was nothing to protect, however, my first days at school soon bought me into conflict with myself. I was bullied, bashed, teased and laughed at. So, classically, and probably following my father's role model, I toughened up, at least on the surface.

The day I finally got in touch with my inner child was one I will never, ever forget. For those of you who never lost your inner child, this must sound pathetic. However, having lost a part of myself so deeply, a part I didn't even know existed, only to find it and realise how precious it is to me, well even now, brings tears.

I began to recognise him. Not in myself, but in others who had looked at me with love and I never understood why. I recognised him in the eyes of a Native American Shaman who had waved eagle feathers in my face. I recognised him in the looks my children gave me at night when I put them to bed and in the eyes of my now ex- wife when we stood to be married. I recognised my inner child in the eyes of the Healer in Indonesia, the Zen monk in Japan, the Yoga teacher, and the priest at my Sunday school.

Suddenly I understood what was so lovable about Chris, something I had never understood before. It was the part of myself that I thought needed fixing, or at least, hiding. It also explained the pain of my divorce from a woman I had long ago stopped feeling love for. She had become the caretaker of my inner child, a place to put it while I went out and - "unburdened" with that vulnerability - played life to the edge. It was such a weird thing to take her for granted for so long, and then not be able to live a day without her.

So, my job became to learn to love this child within me. As simple as it sounds, it wasn't at all. I had the habit of giving it away, and that was the first obstacle. As soon as I'd get cosy with myself I'd find a woman to share him with and try to find new caretaking. That didn't work well. Then I started to parade him around, becoming the 'all spiritual new age guy', soft and vulnerable but that didn't work either because I was a businessman and there's a time and place when that energy just confuses people. So, it took the patience of a loving therapist to stay with me through all these permutations and combinations of how to live with my new self-awareness.

The process of finding him turned out to be relatively easy, compared with the journey of learning how to look after him and what to do with him. I was in the process of a huge divorce and I wanted my ex-wife back. I was having more ups and downs than a yoyo because I didn't know how to look after him. That child inside that I had given to my wife and said, metaphorically, "Look after this part of me please, because it gets in the way of my career, my business, my life."

In my counselling sessions it became obvious that I was still trying to give my child to my ex-wife. My counsellor said, "Now we have met your child, maybe we can find somewhere safer for him until you are ready to look after him yourself". She offered to be the caretaker, but this didn't feel right for some reason.

The solution was, in my opinion one of the most wonderful pieces of human therapy I had and have ever experienced. I found a the most remarkable old tree in the centre of Sydney's Botanical Gardens, climbed it and placed my inner child, my spirit, up there for safe keeping. After several more months in counselling I went back to that park and climbed up into that tree (I was 34), picked up my little spirit and placed him deep into my heart. As I did he woke, smiled, and from that day to now has guided my life, every step. I won't type a keynote without his presence inside me (I never put him on display); I share his happiness with everyone I meet. I give him space from those who would not understand his beauty and I never - never, give him away. Never again.

It was the beginning of my spiritual path. I suddenly knew the difference between being in the world but not of it. There was something precious - my essence - I couldn't change, fix, modify, use, sell or entertain. I found my spirit, my inner child. The next few years were spent getting to know him, learning to love him. Suddenly there was a quietness to life. Suddenly there was a beautiful awareness that if my child was safe I could go anywhere I chose. I was free to be content in the world without a lover to make me so.

This spirit sits inside every human, an inner child. To connect with this spirit go and pick up a child in your arms under the age of three. Let them fall asleep in your arms and, in those moments when they are just closing their eyes, feel that beautiful energy that comes from them. Just when their little ego stops struggling to have more ice cream, or more milk, or more toys, or more something; just when they really stop wanting, there is the spirit of the child. This is like the child within. Your spirit.

A sacred relationship is one in which this child is shared with someone. It must be welcomed. It must be safe in your arms and then you must feel safe in your lover's arms. This child is not a toy. It is a sleeping beauty that gets awakened with a kiss. It is a simple stillness that feels tender and gentle, wants for nothing, and feels content in your arms and safe with your lover.

The ego is built to cover that child (spirit) and eradicate the vulnerability of it. The ego is built to be in the world without that child. We learn tricks like giving that vulnerability away by handing our inner child to someone; "Look after this for me while I go off to work". This is the conventional way to have a relationship, but it makes relationships sick. Hiding that child to make it safe from your lover is even sicker. This is just judging your own worthiness for love. Your spirit, your inner child, is what makes you complete. It doesn't need anything except for you to love it, want it, and it doesn't deserve to be handed over. There is nothing your spirit has done or not done that isn't worthy of love.

When I do a consultation with a person I always meet them first for an interview. I listen to their inner voice, the child's voice within. This is where my guidance begins. It doesn't matter if that person cannot hear what is going on within them, but I must feel that child, that spirit within them, and then I can hear the truth that is being blocked.

When I travel to Nepal I sit on the top of Dream Mountain. A place where I believe any dream that begins from and includes the inner child comes true. I take my child everywhere I go and here on this mountain, he sings. He sings to the angels from whom he came, he sings of love and sunshine. He is my angel; he is my love, never lonely while I am with him.

I take clients to this home in the clouds and by the time they reach this place they are ready. Their child speaks, their heart opens, and their dreams are known. This vision quest isn't a formal thing. The spirit sings from here, on the highest mountains, and the entire world hears the echo. On this mountain in Nepal, Dream Mountain, our spirit surfaces and the ego steps aside.

Think of what you dislike or hate most about yourself. Now think about your childhood and if this part of you always caused you to suffer. You will begin to know your inner child. It is the most precious pearl. Nature wrapped this special secret inside a package for safe keeping, protecting it, to soften its hardships. Nature wrapped it in your ego. Are you ready to open the gift?

A precious pearl – The seat of inspiration.

Treat this wonderful spirit within you, this child, as the precious pearl. Value it more than your life, more than anything. Feel the beauty of it, know that it is not frail; just recognise how precious it is. Grown from the belly of a shell deep in the ocean from a single grain of sand. Your spirit. It wants nothing, needs nothing, and therefore has everything.

Now, unwrap it from that silk cloth you call protection. Remove the coverings, and another, and another. Get past the idea that someone wants to steal it and unwrap another layer again. Learn to care for it, find a safe place to keep it within you and make a promise that wherever you go, she or he comes with you, and if it is not there, you are not there. It's not a burden carrying around so don't hand it to someone else.

Your inner spirit does not fear, you do. Your inner child is not wrong or stupid, you are. There is nothing that can damage it, nothing you can change. Nothing can hurt your inner self; nothing can hurt your love. Only your ego can be damaged. There is nothing that can hurt your inner spirit. Only our ego can try to deny it's existence and then we become inauthentic, uninspired.

That is always the great discovery of self-help. In the end, there is no self to help. There is only love.

Chapter 13. Witnessing Miracles
The Universal Laws of Nature

If there is one thing that I've been gifted to celebrate in my work it is the witnessing of miracles. Those are not the spooky types of miracles, they are everyday miracles.

Miracles do happen and the ability to see them is simply a matter of your consciousness. To a person in their lower mind, a car accident might be a devastating event; or to a person going through a divorce there might seem like total disaster. However, by applying the laws of nature, universal law, those events become different. From the most catastrophic circumstance comes a flower, a new awareness and that is the miracle.

We are often prevented from witnessing the miracle of life because of our emotional attachments, or our cultural beliefs that essentially block higher mind perspective. An example might be theft. We might consider that theft is all bad because the victim lost and the thief gained. However, the victim gained and the thief lost too. Nothing exists in that original emotional universe of loss without gain. Only in the human psyche, the ego mind.

I have been gifted to take thousands of people to the depth of their soul, unconditional love. It is a miraculous journey because in the end, what seemed to be a bundle of chaotic drama that caused untold pain was actually also a blessing. It was both good and bad. It is within this consciousness of observation, seeing the two sides one can see the miracle of life. Nothing is random.

There was once a great mirror called "the Mysteries". To look in that magical mirror was to look into the wisdom of all creation. One could understand what was meant by "the love of God". In this mirror, creation was broken into seven sacred steps called the seven realms. The earth was the first realm, the moon the second, the sun the forth, and the edge of the solar system the seventh. The forth realm, the sun, was defined as the highest love that our physical senses could perceive. It was called the "heart of man". This fourth realm was known as the highest level of comprehension possible in our life and, therefore, the highest realm the physical human could understand. It was called "God."

One day, that mirror was shattered. Fragments were scattered. The books were burned, the knowledge outlawed. People ran and picked up those fragments and held them up saying, "Look I have found the truth", but they held only a fragment and they called these fragments the religions of earth. So the great teachings became a mystery, secretly handed down by word of mouth. This is what I am sharing with you, if you are ready. The laws of nature are, in fact, the ancient mysteries, retold in modern language.

It is a simple story, that greatest story. It is defined in the Bible, in Hindu texts, it is understood in every language, in stories of dragons and birds, of eagles. It is drawn on rock, built in statues (pyramids), and told in folklore. The seven primal states of human behaviour reveal it - the evolution of our species from amoeba to human. The story is retold a thousand million times. It is the story of love. How life works and why.

The Universal Laws of Nature – Witnessing the miracle.

Nature is the keeper of sacred law. Witness her life and compare it. She is the guardian of reality. Our expectations of nature are for her to be her best; to be strong, to change, to be calm and to surrender. To be born and to die, and in her existence, to evolve.

Since the forest is the keeper of sacred law it is a worthy beginning to ask her to share principles of reality. The forest, the ocean, the sky, species, plants animals and insects all have a voice. It will require the deepest silence to hear it, that place you are invited to observe sacred moments.

By living as nature intended and following her laws you are actually moving emotion to love. By applying her five magnificent perspectives you can see through life, rather than at it.

1. The law of balance – There are two sides to everything.

2. The law of growth – The purpose of everything is growth.

3. The law of interconnectedness – Nothing is missing just changes in form.

4. The law of harmony – What you appreciate grows.

5. The law of hierarchy – As above so below.

1. The first law of nature is that everything seeks balance.

It is a self-evident fact that everything that is free in nature seeks balance.

If one single atom in the entire universe were out of balance the whole of creation would be destroyed. Nature expresses this law of balance by continually seeking it. Growth and decay, birth and death, weather, tides successes and failure are all the manifestation of this greater law. All in the universe seeks balance, and without it, all would self-destruct.

Look around in this wondrous space and take careful note. All creation is drawn to be spherical. The earth is round. The sun is round. The planets are round. The solar system is round. A radius reaching out from the sun in all directions would describe the interior of a hollow globe. If you drop hot lead through the air it takes a round shape as it falls. All matter seeks the same shape and no power exists in the universe that can alter the tendency.

Conflict only exists when people take a self-determined and earthly perspective of imbalanced thought. We call this stress, conflict or war, and it exits in the form of emotion. Emotions exist when a person aspires to defy nature by trusting their thinking in contrast to nature. To create a good without it's correlate wrong, an upper without it's correlate downer. Stress is caused by imbalance. All stress comes from the mind, a way of thinking, the choices we make. What sickness is not the result of a stubborn hold on imbalanced thinking? What war and boundary between nations is not divided on the basis of imbalanced ideals? We build prisons of beliefs and then fight to remain inside them.

The first law of nature gives you the freedom to lead of a life of truth rather than illusion.

If you can't manage your emotions you can't manage your business, finances and relationship. So the understanding of the dynamic that there are two sides to everything translates to human emotions. Instead of trying to eradicate things in your life that cannot be eradicated you can instead become appreciative of them. In a sense, it is the law of balance the gives you the true sense of Personal Harmony.

All distresses and bankruptcies come from misunderstanding of this law. Chasing rainbows or being drawn into short-term emotional investments is the consequence of unbalanced thinking. The law of balance also helps to develop mental stability and maturity in relationships. It alleviates mental health problems and is instrumental in creating a balanced body structure.

In summary, first law of nature is that everything seeks balance, revealing that without ego, I will admit and respect that if I am beautiful, I must also be ugly. If I am clever, I must also be dumb. If I am sensible, I must also be silly. If I am wise, I must also be ignorant. If I am poor, I must also be wealthy. If I am spiritual, I must also be human. If I am anything then I must also be its opposite in some other area of my life. Balance is an attractive quality; it radiates and brings with it an air of confidence and integrity. Law number one is about humility to the balance if nature. Metaphysically, Balance is harmony and harmony is love. This is our true nature. Balanced thinking is, therefore, essential to having an open heart.

2. The second law of nature – Growth.

"Everything flows, out and in: Everything has tides: All things rise and fall: the pendulum swing manifests in everything: the measure of the swing to the right is the measure of the swing to the left: Rhythm compensates."

The Kyabalion.

That everything in nature has a purpose is self-evident. When we are in tune with that rhythm, our purpose, we feel gratitude, presence, certainty and love. This is what people are searching for all over the world, and it comes naturally when we finally become aware of the intention, the bigger picture of our lives. Life is meant to be lived with great happiness and this happiness must be experienced in context. If we are always viewing our life from a self-interest position, we are always healing and growing, never content. So grasping this last law is the pinnacle of self-development, finding a cause, a passion and love for something bigger than us. This is the key to happiness.

The second law of nature is that of evolution. Maximum evolution occurs at the border of chaos and order. Therefore, all things must grow and grow best with a magnificent blend of both challenge and support.

This challenge and support can come invited, or not. Your business and your life both evolve along the border of chaos and order. You can't avoid the law because it is universal. However, you are free to consciously choose challenge rather than avoid it.

Nature never grows continuously. She grows in surges, and your business and life will also grow in surges. It means there will be times of quiet and some semblance of calm, and then there will be periods of chaos. The conscious individual will stimulate their life with chaos on a daily basis. In other words, they will invite or even create challenge, and at the same token, in their daily life they will create calm and tranquillity. The more an organisation can embrace both, and welcome them equally, the more it will stay on track and, therefore, the more profitable it becomes.

3. The third law of nature - Interconnectedness.

6,000 years of the study of consciousness brings us the awareness that the separations we create cause all our pain. In trying to protect and identify ourselves, we become imprisoned. Loving a few, ignoring the rest. To reconnect and dismantle this false identity. You need to go where the ego cannot travel and challenge your beliefs. If you can take this journey and travel back to where the roots of your real self exist, somewhere deep into your heart and soul, you will break the mould and actually live what most people dream. Open and outside that self-imposed prison. Try it. Try loving everyone.

It's a journey of peeling away the layers, a journey of cutting through the myths, the ideas, the intellect and all the mind stuff that has accumulated to create your ego. A journey on which you peel back centuries of ideas and experiences, built as layers over the truth that happens in one single sacred moment, and totally and absolutely fall, without shame, in love with life itself.

These skills sustain love for a lifetime. We can slice through the baggage that prevents us from sustaining a sacred and beautiful reality of love every single day our entire life.

The journey is not for the faint hearted. There is no sugar coating on this gift. There is no self-development new age mumbo jumbo. 6,000 years of the Mysteries of Love, and the thousands of great minds who devoted their lives to understanding it, deserves to be shared without puffery. If a sustainable, sacred, ego free loving life is what you want then follow nature as your guide. It is awe inspiring and transformative.

We separate into football clubs, religions, music genre, clothing types, sports, diet groups (vegetarians), belief systems, colour, gender, race, wealth etc. This self-protective identification is totally understandable. We join clubs that give us a sense of safety and being wanted. Some are weird, some are anti-social, but we join whatever makes us feel wanted and in the process of doing so, we lose our soul.

To really know yourself, you have to pull down the barriers and see that everyone is really part of the same family.

The third law of nature is the law of interconnectedness. What it means is that all things on earth are interconnected. Everything is managed by the nature of vibration. The third law implies that anything I see in myself I must be able to find in another person, or what I see in others, I must find in myself. We are all interconnected with each other and with nature. What we do ourselves - thought, word and deed - we do to the world and visa versa.

Given this awareness one can make an extraordinary discovery, "Nothing is ever missing it just changes in form". That means that there cannot be a death, only a change in form. This is a powerful belief of the American Indian and Australian Aboriginal. That when we leave the body we simply change form. Even the Bible talks of it. So our attachment to life breeds our grief of death. But according to this law, there is no death, just a change in form.

The value of this law in an organisational sense is in conflict management or conflict resolution. Interpersonal conflicts cost companies and individuals huge amounts of personal and corporate time. As the pace of life increases, so the value of that time has increased. The essential nature of conflict is not that it is, but that it can be, productive. It is also inevitable. Honouring diversity means the awareness of differences. This awareness means conflict can be understood and dealt with differently.

4. The fourth law of nature is the law of harmony.

When we contemplate and learn to become one with nature, our hearts open to its music. We say, "I enjoyed nature", but what is it in nature that we enjoy? The rhythmic movement, the perfect harmony of nature - a harmony that can be lost in the artificial life, has touched something in us. This is the real temple, the true religion. . If we are in tune with our self and the rhythms of nature, then one moment standing in the midst of nature with an open heart is like a lifetime of fulfilment.

A lack of harmony has disastrous effects on the world. All the troubles on our earth come from this dissymmetry including all the tragedy inside each individual and the multitudes. Harmony is best produced in one's own life. We see that the world today needs it more than ever. Perhaps there will come a time when nature's law and its philosophy become the religion of humanity.

The beat and pulse of the heart are harmonious. The inhalation and exhalation of our breath are the result of a continuous rhythm and tempo. All life depends upon this musical pattern. The breath manifests as voice, word and sound. This internal harmony, with its dependence on a perpetual cadence of notes, echoes the sound of a perfect song from the harmony found in the world around us. This is creation at work.

The fourth law of nature is the law of harmony. What determines the quality and quantity of the life force of any one individual is the level of gratitude in their thoughts. All thoughts are electric; they send electrical charges to the nerves, which in turn stimulate action. The quality of your thoughts is determined by the quality of your appreciation. Judgments create ingratitude; ingratitude compresses and shrinks life. Getting into abundance and the future demands an appreciation of what has passed, so it's no longer an affect on the future. This is the value of this fourth law.

This law creates the opportunity for an organisation to create a culture of growth an appreciation. What you appreciate grows and, therefore, an organisational culture based on the law of harmony will evolve rapidly along the border of chaos and order. This provides an opportunity to build teamwork around business vision and purpose. Ingratitude on the other hand destroys not only businesses, but also the individuals within it. To understand the law of harmony is to understand human relationship. It is a way to think and be that can inspire incredible human spirit.

5. The fifth law is the Law of The one and the Many.

The fifth law of Nature gives us a huge and magnificent perspective on life. To understand nature's perspective on life, we sit on the moon and look back at our magnificent planet. Then all he embraces, shares and gives hold us in awe; it is easy to be impressed at the beauty of life. We are objective because nothing affects us. We can no longer associate with good or bad, right or wrong. Our footy team doesn't really matter from way out here, we have a balanced perspective, and a smile comes over our face. Wow! We can see the whole magnificent story of human existence, including our own, spinning on that globe. The traumas and wars just seem part of something bigger. The overall picture becomes important, events become like the fallen leaves of a great tree, just a part of the evolution of life. This is the perspective given to us through the Universal law of Balance.

And now we descend back toward earth and begin to see borders and nations, conflicts and disturbances in isolation. Our perspective shifts from a global one to a local one. Back into our ego, we finally land, feet back on the earth. That perspective, so easily achieved on the moon, is quickly lost now, because our new perspective is a personal one. But we don't quite fully descend do we? We don't land here innocent. We will argue, "This is right and this is wrong", because now, as a grain of sand on a huge beach of sand grains, we fear our lack of importance. We poke our head up out of the sand grains around us and say, "Hey, you bastards look at me. I'm Chris. I'm clever. I'm rich. I'm famous. I'm right. I'm spiritual". We grab a little bubble of ideas and try to make ourselves bigger than a grain of sand.

Now we are grains of sand in bubbles. Neither free to be a grain of sand and enjoy it, nor free to be on the moon and be in awe of it. Now we are grains of sand with bubbles called ego, and we think the more of something we are, the better we are. What total and absolute rubbish. No matter how big that bubble, you're still a grain of sand. And one high tide will prove it so.

Now, as grain of sand we cannot see the whole, we can only see our part of the beach. We see our home, our family, our work, our friends, and our enemies. And our opinion, which on the moon was irrelevant and inconsequential, now becomes the golden truth. The bubble we call ourselves is now constructed with ideas, thoughts and materials. We read newspapers and magazines, attend courses and church, looking to reinforce and justify our personal perspective on the world, "This is good" or "This is bad". Until the tide comes in. This is the ego perspective.

This journey demonstrates the difference between the higher mind perspective and the lower mind perspective. We choose the one we use to see the world around us.

The forces involved in the government of nature and her worlds are mighty in their power, yet humble in obedience. They must conform. We've seen lightning leap across the sky and tear its way into the earth, seemingly following some movement that was due to chance. Yet every scientist who has studied lightning knows that it obeys a fixed rule in all it's activities and it will never deviate from that rule.

The sun gives out original light and is the master of our solar system. No planets do this; they are obedient to the sun. They are travelling around their sun and cannot get away. They go just so far out into space and then get pulled back. Even distance is not relevant in space, the laws of nature that operate here on earth still hold true. Everything in the universe reports to natural law. Obedience is the nature of things.

All things have a central power that controls them. This is a self-evident law. There never was or could be a tribe that did not have its chief. Nor has there been a city or a town without a mayor or leader. There is never a body of people that is without a leader. All businesses have them.

There is an order in the chaos that we call life. There are local laws, cultural laws and religious laws. And governing all these laws are nature's laws. The law of the one and the many. Many people follow – one or two lead. Many people believe what they hear but only one or two question it. While many people are at the mercy of media, emotion and mass consciousness, one or two step beyond it.

The leader, the entrepreneur, the artist, the performer, the inventor and the inspired parent each function outside the conventions of the many. They question, they remain humble to a vision, an inspiration or a sense of purpose. The real liberation comes when we tap this gift and step into the guidance of nature.

Chapter 14. Your Constitution True Nature

When we are committed to self-awareness, self-knowledge, what self are we referring to? The one that likes blueberry ice cream? Or the one that wants $1,000,000 in the bank? Are we referring to the self that is no self, the higher mind, and if so, what is there to know? That self has no personality or identity.

There is a self that you can know that doesn't change from birth to death. It is not your Ego mind, or your personality; it cannot be measured by your success, fame, drama or achievements in life. It is a soul template and it is called your personal constitution.

Stereotyping human beings has been the desire of the confused for many thousands of years, classing people by race, colour, religion or gender has been the game of cruelty since time began. However, there is a way to understand our nature that is not based on segregating or making one group more important or better than the rest. That is your constitution.

It is best to describe your constitution with an example that puts the topic at arms length. Let's say you buy a Volkswagen car – a Beatle. It's one of the great cars of the last century and is a fun little "Bug" – one day, your friend calls and says "can you help me, I need to plough my farm and I need to borrow your car" I suspect you'd become protective of your VW and politely refuse. The next day another friend rings up "can I borrow your car, I am racing in a formula one grand prix and my Ferrari broke down (again). That wouldn't work either would it?

So, with the body shape, engine type and chassis frame we determine the "best use" for our car. Yet, we humans occupy a sort of body shape, engine type and chassis frame of our own, and that also could be give the classification of "best use."

A person with big bones might well want to do the high jump in the Olympic games but I suspect nature has designed that frame for the shot put, or wrestling match. There's nothing to stop that big boned person trying for the Olympic High Jump but I wonder if they are flying against what nature intended, rather than working with it?

Self-knowledge is this. To understand the machine you've inhabited on this visit to earth and see that it is built for certain perfect and sustainable functions. It therefore must be treated, like our VW, with respect and care. But not like everyone else's. They might occupy a Ford, or a Jeep. So, what they eat, how they live, what they do to become inspired, might be completely different to you. Now it gets interesting right?

In the ancient mysteries, the source of my Laws of Nature, there is a firm belief that you, the soul, inhabit a certain type of 'machine frame" in order for you to do what is intended for you on this visit. So, the Soul template is created, within the womb of the mother, before you occupy it. You choose the frame based on the journey you, the soul, need to take on this visit to earth.

Now we, the mind part, sit in total confusion watching this story going "hey, what about me?" – and we'll get to that. The frame, chassis and engine are created and our soul enters it at birth. The only part we haven't included yet, it's you, the mind. Let's call it the lower mind and the middle minds - Emotional, mental and sensory capacities - these are inherited from the parents, and are developable by the individual throughout their life; this is called your consciousness.

So, the last cog in this wheel. Why? Why do it like this? And the mysteries again have the answer. All the lower and middle minds want, really want, is to return home, back to unite with the higher mind, you, the Soul. So, they spend their whole existence searching for something. For new clothes, new foods, new sports, new mountains to climb, new loves, new lovers: looking under every bush, looking for life, but really searching for love, the seat of the Soul.

Some people commit suicide trying to get out of the pain of that search because they thought they found home, but it wasn't. Some people get ill because they are tired of searching and just want a break. Other people build multi billion empires trying to delay the inevitable realization that they didn't find what they were looking for. Others get addicted to drugs in the hope that the search will go away. There are others, most interestingly who think that being in a body and having a mind is a total burden to the search and they use spirituality to escape the confines of the mind, but that doesn't work either. The real soul mate, the real success story every human being wants, is to re unite with themselves, their lower mind, middle mind and higher mind as one. From whence they came.

That's called God. It's semantics to worry about the label. Simply said it means unity. It means that the lower mind searching for pleasure, or the middle mind searching for love and acceptance, can never be happy for long.

They are really looking for substitutes along a path that can only end in connection with our Soul. The story is told in so many fables, like the resurrection of Jesus from the cave. It's like we all come to earth, hang around wishing we were back home with Dad, finally, we leave the body we inhabited, and return. The only thing potently different about Jesus is that he knew it. We don't. So, he was enlightened.

It's one reason why consumerism doesn't work. No matter how much we get, how much we are happy when we get it, we're never satisfied. The real satisfaction is beyond the senses. However, like a tree, we can't put special leaves right on the tips of branches, if there's no trunk, or roots. We can't get enlightened without real life, a body and a mind all lined up in harmony. So, if this story inspires you to take a short cut like the hippies tried, let me assure you, it doesn't work. You can't fly home without your luggage being processed through the scanner.

When you love life, all life, every bit of life, you get through stage one scanner. When you can manifest material, spiritual, financial, sexual, relationship success in life, then you get through the second scanner. When you can teach it, give it, and share it with others you get through the third and final scanner. As Jesus, Buddha, Moses and Mohamed did, just to name a few of the many.

So, inspiration is not just about "feeling great" it's about winning a ticket to the greatest lottery of all, love, heart mind and Soul.

Your constitution limits your process. We can tell the constitution of a baby before it is born so, your personality and trophies, and the way you act, don't have anything to do with your constitution. Your constitution is about the sort of machine, you and your personality mind have occupied.

Self-knowledge is about this machine. If you can work with it, you can have a wonderful healthy life. If you work against it, you'll be grabbing for substitutes like: sexuality, greed, substance and spirituality (Yoga, etc) for the whole of your life looking for what nature already gave you.

What kills most people is trying to be someone they are not. That's sad. For example, a fire constitution is usually bad at managing things. They build things, change things, but when it comes to maintenance, that is a disaster. Let's say a fire person falls in love. They get into a relationship but their partner resists change. What now? Either the fire goes out, call this chronic fatigue, burnout, exhaustion, alcoholism or adrenal failure or, the fire person finds a job where they can do, fire. But what if they have a job as an accountant? Depending on consistency, regularity and the ability to remain stable. Now, the fire is like gelignite, and this fire person is going to self-destruct.

Then they think, "Oh, my life is out of balance, I must calm this fire" and immediately kill their harmony, eventually cause cancer, and die. Alcoholics, criminals, violent people are often Fire people who don't like their fire and therefore don't have a healthy path for their life.

We self delude around this topic. For example, I have a friend whose body constitution is Earth. That person is so grounded. They are perfect at doing repetitive, reliable things, and they are so strong like a tractor. They could move a mountain if they had to. The difficulty they have is that they think their way of doing life is the best way. Obviously for them it is, but for a long skinny beanpole ether constitution person, that'd kill them. If an ether constitution starts copying an earth person's way of life, that's suicide to inspiration in days.

Water people love caring. From nursing staff caring for the sick, Oprah Winfrey caring for the world, and to the front row of a rugby grid caring for the other members of the team. Those Water people are amazing caregivers. Yet, they go on health programs and diets to try to be someone else. That's like taking God's gift and shoving it in his nose. If we are a certain constitution we'd better live it out of respect for ourselves and for the creator.

Water people try to be like Air people, Fire people want to be like Water people, Ether people don't know who they want to be like, and Air people think they are like everyone. Earth people stay out of the debate and just get on with making more money or managing the mess we all left behind.

The science of human constitution is profound. It is 6,000 years old and most practitioners, like Ayurvedic doctors and Deepak Chopra have bent it to make it fit western ideals. Real Constitutional Analysis says, "find your constitution and live it" whereas western adaptations say "find your constitutions and kill it – by seeking balance and peace" that's a train wreck waiting to happen.

Would you tell a cat to become a dog? Would you fill a Ferrari with standard petrol? Would you give a fire person vegetarian diets? Would you feed an etheric person meat? This is food for thought, and there is more on this topic below.

Body types.

The five elements are Ether, Air, Fire, Water and Earth. We all have these five elements within us and the proportions of each one vary from person to person. Those proportions never change, from the moment of birth to death. No matter how much we eat or exercise, read or don't read, the proportions never change. This is called you Elemental Constitution.

I will summarise these body types here for you, but in my book "Innerwealth 4;" this is explained in great detail and includes a self-analysis for you to determine your Element.

- Earth People – Stocky
- Water People – Round and fleshy
- Fire people – Medium muscular
- Air People – Short thin
- Ether – Tall thin

EARTH

Do you know me? I am Earth I have a strong square frame, people say I'm heavy boned for my size. I can be tall, I can be short, but the general opinion is that I am stocky, strong. Build for strength and hard work. The consequence of my strong frame is that: I love the home we build and the safety. I love the security and the trust we share. I am strong yet, fragile. Controlling, you might think, but I act to make our world safe. I am the earth - reality is my level. I hold fast to all that is tangible and I am lost like a child in all that is not. I am bricks and mortar; I am money in the hand. I am security and trust.

WATER

Do you know me? I am Water. My body is heavy boned too, just like earth, but I have soft muscle tissue, people describe my body as soft, rounded. My frame is quite large however; so don't mistake me for an overweight person on a skinny frame. I do have a larger, rounded frame. To me, Love is easy to give, I nurture. I am the healer who can give and give.

FIRE

Do you know me? I am Fire. My body looks pretty good, athletic, even if I don't work out. My body is average frame size but the muscle is rarely soft. I have tenacity in my frame, fast and strong. Because of this body frame: I love to be the best, win every test. I like anything competitive and will even turn my yoga class into a competition. I am insatiable yet not inexhaustible. I am fired up one moment and feeling burned out the next. My love is expressed in my action.

AIR

Do you know me? I am Air. I'm easy to recognize because I am shorter than the average person in my culture. Usually my bones are thin, fragile, and small and I have thin ankles and wrists. Sometimes I have fat surrounding me, but it's the frame you need to observe. My fingers are thin too. Because of my body frame I am like a bird, always moving, pecking at this, learning that, picking up tips, dropping off seeds. I love diversity, multi tasking and I'm often late because I think of more things to do while I am on the way. I am creative, inventive and always trying new things.

ETHER

Do you know me? I am Ether. I am easy to recognize because I am tall for my culture. I don't always come in skinny packets. Sometimes I am mixed with earth and look like a giant, but pure me, Ether is just plain tall and usually, quite bony. I am the visionary, I can see for miles ahead. Sadly, that makes being in the moment nearly impossible. If you ask me to do that, I'll drift off into the future. I often turn to the mystical, my angels and my Gods for help. I sometimes choose partners unwisely because I get ungrounded and they help for a while.

Your Natural Constitution

Written By Rama Prasad and Chris Walker

Your Natural Constitution is unique to you and each constitution has its own special way of existing healthily. So the day of generic diets, one office fitting everyone, mass trends in colour and style is at last a thing of the past. Your True Nature is absolutely unique and needs to be treated that way. Five different elements of nature, earth, water, fire, air and ether, result in five different paths: five trends, five office styles, five diets, five lifestyles, five music styles and millions of combinations in between. But rather than make life more complex, they totally allow you to design your world so your True Nature has a perfect home without thinking your style, your way, fits everyone.

This way of seeing nature also allows you to balance your life depending on your circumstance. In consitutional lifestyles you eat, sleep, drink, do yoga, play sport, make love according to your constitution, and you adjust those things to sustain equilibrium. Excess or deficiency cause illness and disease, so we play in life according to a sense of wellbeing.

This is in stark contrast to the mundane ideas of one yoga class suits all people, or one meditation, or one medicine. That idea is negative and demoralizing. If a fire person doesn't do fire life, they explode in rage and self-aggression. Yet, if a water person tries to emulate the fire person, they'll shrink into depression.

So, constitutional lifestyles bring your True Nature out into the world in the best, healthiest and most productive way. This we call spirituality and we adjust it according to circumstance. If your Water constitution is in excess, demonstrated by fluid retention and excess weight, you'll be able to find the Water reduction lifestyle and all will be fine. It's a personalized way of living. It no longer wishes to clone you by saying you "SHOULD" do this and SHOULD do that. It simply offers you your Natural Constitution –your birthright – with all its idiosyncrasies and then your "Behavioural Constitution" with all its imbalances and outcomes. You dial up the change and make subtle adjustments as required. The implication is that one ideology, one diet, one motivation, one value set fits all is for mass consciousness, and you need a more aware process for life than that.

Your 'constitution' – reveals the weather you thrive in, the foods to balance you, the exercise that suits you and the career you can live in harmony with. It reveals your possible imbalances and potential vulnerabilities and cautions you on what your potential lifestyle hazards are.

It is like sculpting. There before you sits a rock, rough and covered in mud. You begin to chip away at its surface and slowly, through hard work, you find a beautiful sculpture within it.

Our constitution is exactly like the potential that sits within this rock. Through training we need to remove the unwanted bits and discover the gem that lies within it. The first thing is to understand what is your Natural Constitution, which is the exact shape of that gem. To do this we examine the body you were born into. Then we reveal how it responds to the world around it. How it is meant to care for itself and what its natural process in life is. In other words we learn what it takes to honor who we really are in our most natural state.

By Rama Prasad

Your Constitution In Brief

Ether	Tranquillity, peace, freedom, stillness, calmness, openness, wisdom and creativity.
Air	Rhythm, response, movement, cycles, flow, detachment (positive) and changeable.
Fire	Courage, analysis, solution, speed, transformation, drive, passion, intensity, heat and force.
Water	Love, compassion, connection, flexibility, attachment (positive) caring and sharing.
Earth	Stability, support, reliability, grounding, establishment, firmness and solidity.

How Your Constitution Functions

Ether Predominant.

Ether people are tall and thin boned.

Perspective is ether's gift. Ether people see the world from a long way off and therefore have an amazing sense of fantasy and possibility. Ether people love space. Both physically in homes that are open and airy, and personally, thriving on lots of time alone.

Ether people are rarely hampered by reality and we should be careful to support them in their fantasies and dreaming. It is this great asset that they bring to the world of business and family, providing often surreal, but always imaginative visions of the future.

If it is time to expand your sense of possibility in life, find yourself an ether person and ask their opinion. It is usually astronomical.

As a result of this almost otherworldly skill, Ether people are often hard to understand. Their sense of time is rarely accurate and their own attention to detail is poor (such details tend to stifle the ether imagination).

Philosophical by nature, Ether people need the space to dream, write, paint and think. They are creative and are known to overwhelm those whose duty it is to make practical sense of their ideas, because they never stop imagining.

Inspiration is the realm dominated by the Ether people. When each of us, no matter what our constitutional strengths, need to reach into the worlds of vision, inspiration and purpose, we must tap our own resource of ether. To do this we simply eat, find the space, and embrace the lifestyle constitution of the ether person.

Ether people tend to overuse their ether in life. Excessive reading, excessive thinking and excessive planning agitate ether. When this happens, Ether people can make no sense at all. They can become ungrounded, highly emotional and self-deprecating, during which time, they are always ready for a quarrel. The solution in these unbalanced times, is to put water, or earth lifestyle around them.

Another potential problem for most Ether people is that they get trapped in their head and forget about all practicalities. They can become unreliable and often spaced out with too many options on their mind. They are often anxious, easily worried, and many thoughts pass through their heads in a short space of time. Ethers often worry themselves to an early death. Being anxious, they also might also be prone to strokes and heart attacks.

The ether person, who chooses to stay in balance with his Constitution, will surround himself with the following support.

1. Earthy advisors and coaches (Ether people often gravitate to ether advice, which is like petrol on a fire)

2. Space – physical and emotional (in order to think)

3. Stillness – meditation, swimming and walking

4. Regularity in food, food quality, snacks that are healthy and abstinence from stimulants (smoking, nicotine substitutes, coffee, tea, alcohol, drugs)

5. Respect for the real world issues of being on time (early for appointments) and predictability

Environmentally, Ether people cope badly with extremes such as heat, cold and wind. From a medical perspective, these ethers have an 'unstable metabolism.' The digestive organs are their most vulnerable region. The large intestine, brain and nervous system are most at risk. They often get circulatory problems.

Ether thrives on tranquillity. It needs peace, space and freedom in order to manifest. Ether predominant people are often their own greatest enemies, attracted to interesting things like a moth to a flame but they are often disturbed by their own inquisitive nature. Ether evolves from stillness so in order for your etheric character to come forward you'll need to create meditative space and personal mind control to bring it to the world.

Ether can be silent in meetings and at home because they are conversing in their heads. They are dreaming the reality, rather than facing it. Ether is one solution to personal trauma.

Ether also thrives on silence – the music of the universe, silence. But soothing, gentle, meaningful classical piano is also etheric by nature. The sounds of nature are Ether's heart. This together with the colour white and other very natural pastel colours make Ether environments a very sacred place to be.

Famous Ether predominant people are Goliath, God, Edmund Hillary, Elle McPherson, Mohamed Ali, Nicole Kidmann, Kerry Packer (has all 5 constitutions strong) Rumi, Socrates, Cleopatra, Hermes, Pythagorus, Columbus, Pattanjali, and most NBL Basketball players.

Air Predominant.

Air People are small and thin boned.

The gift of the Air person is connection. Air is the bridge between the etheric world of fantasy and the real world of experience. Air people thrive on complexity, their ability to link and conceptualise events and ideas is an amazing asset.

Air people are the most creative. Their gift is in huge demand in environments where people need diverse possibilities and potential brought under some control. In the world of concepts, Air people weave the web that links opportunity with possibility.

The complexity of life is in essence its beauty. The multiplicity of shapes and forms, and colours and objects all interact to create one amazing whole. It's like creating the whole from unrelated parts, the merging of movement, like a dance where diverse talents are harnessed to become one understandable performance.

If it's time to improve, expand and develop through the art of communication, Air people have the gift. They thrive in multi-media, complexity and music and dance-related professions. Air people love to teach their skills. They are the happiest teachers.

You would love to walk with this person, do things with this person and even live with this person –as he would be so easy going, is never stiff with his plans, ideas or likes and dislikes.

Air people tend to over-use the Air constitution in life. Excessive talking, excessive travels and excessive changes can aggravate Air and deprive Air people of the other four constitutions in life. When this imbalance happens the undercurrents are tremendous: minds are busy, anxieties and worries dominate achy bodies, tense muscles, dry skin and blocked thinking result. It gives rise to the expression "air head".

When each of us has an Air imbalance, we can easily fall into frequent fights and we can suffer from poor memory and irregular body rhythms while becoming quite unpredictable. This can lead to anxiety and hypersensitivity. Another potential problem for most Air people is that they can become unreliable and often spaced out with too many options on their mind.

From a medical perspective, Air Predominant people have an 'unstable digestive heat.' The digestive organs are their most vulnerable regions. The large intestine is most at risk as is the heart and they suffer more frequently from vascular disorders and stress-related illnesses. Overall the air type has cold, unstable and very changeable properties, which can vacillate from cold to hot. They are cured and brought back into balance by everything that grounds them and makes them heavier, warmer and more stable.

Healthy Air people love a carefree life. They love to switch between work and play, at will. They need a lot of light, moist and warm food items to maintain health. They need to eat when they are hungry. This is because external factors influence their appetite easily.

The Air person, who chooses to stay in balance in his constitution, will surround himself with the following support.

1. Grounding environments where there is routine (Earth), love (Water), motivation (Fire) and freedom (Ether).

2. Rhythm – a regular daily schedule that is difficult to change.

3. An active environment where their creativity can flourish – dance, art etc.

4. Pleasant music, yellow colours, harmonious conversation with friends. Regular warm oil massages by a supportive, calm and sensitive individual.

5. Warmth of every kind is important including well-heated rooms, warm clothing, warm weather.

Air people live in a world of their own, prioritising things, which seem secondary to everyone else. They are active people who move from one task to another with grace and speed. Air is the constitution of touch- the tangibility of things and people.

Air people need a lifestyle where many opportunities are available even if none are taken. They need to know that there are choices. Air types love to talk and are creatively stifled where conversation is restricted. Air is disturbed by chaos. Too much chaos overwhelms the air constitution spinning it out of control. This includes information which conflicts with either their existing belief set or contradicts previous data.

People love the Air energy. It's a sort of letting go, sharing and a can-do energy. Air people are full of ideas and usually very easygoing for they can change on a dime. Air music is any music that swings, grooves and flows. From Opera to Modern and Latino, anything that is not repetitive and monotonous. Just like the music – air energy loves different colour, stripes spots and patterns.

Mahatma Gandhi and Mother Teresa were Air Predominant people staying 'easy' in the most complex of circumstances.

Fire Predominant.

Strong build, good muscle, average height.

Fire people are gifted with the drive, the passion, the power to change, transform and evolve. Fire people pave the way for new life. Fire is the warrior, the king, the analyst and the strategist. Competition is the keynote of the Fire people. They thrive when there is a challenge and are easily bored when the status quo is unchangeable.

If it is time to grow, change, innovate and improve your world, find a fire person, they will motivate and direct you wisely. When the change is undertaken, remember to let go or you may find yourself and your world under the continual microscope of change, change and more change.

You won't find a more direct – straight to the point constitution than Fire. Fire people love to face difficulties or challenges in life. Known for their courage and passion, Fire people possess the drive. They are able to analyse situations and find solutions so the world of consulting, transformation and preaching has typically brought Fire types to the fore.

Fire people tend to overuse Fire. Excessive analysis, competition, judgment, speed, hot food, excess alcohol and stimulation agitate Fire. When this happens you'll quickly see frustration, rudeness and anger. The warm hearted leadership of Fire gives way to power and force. In these times, to settle their imbalance, they need cooling – fast. This means a Water or Earth lifestyle needs to be injected into the Fire world to slow it, calm it and relax it.

If you want to see the latest technology, visit a Fire office. They love those new gadgets. This is one of their sources of ultimate pleasure. Strong colours bring out Fire and constant feedback and rewards keep the Fire alive.

When each of us loses balance in our Fire constitution, we become acidic, irritable and frustrated. We start to lick our old wounds, ask for apologies and send guilt in all directions. Our anger can take a steep curve toward vengeance and violence if it is left unchecked.

The Fire person, who chooses to stay in balance in his Constitution, will surround himself with the following support.

1. The freedom to move, let go, and find spaces where fire is needed (change).

2. Self Awareness – the ability to understand where Fire is simply not welcome –(healing, people management and human development).

3. Competitive environments – where laziness, lack of drive, confusion and uncertainty don't thrive.

4. Good food, and avoid excess of stimulants of any kind, including sugar, chocolate, wine, coffee and cigarettes.

5. Cool friends and environments that nurture and support recovery.

Fires love a fast, progressing, bright world. They want change, now, here. They love to have a challenging relationship, work and hobbies. Challenge fuels them.

Environmentally, Fire people thrive on a moist, winter climate, green trees, blue water and shades to cool them down. The ideal location for their life would be a waterfall surrounded by tall leafy trees, a cozy cottage with the fastest internet connection and the latest laptop to deal with the international stock market at the flick of a finger. Their choice of holidays will be similar. Beaches, surfs, water sports, snowy mountains and rainforests are their usual destinations. Everywhere awaits the challenges for them. Or else they create them.

Medically speaking, Fire people are weak around their liver, blood, gall bladder, small intestine and heart. This is because most of them overuse heat and hotspots of the body get affected easily. Usually they respond well to the cooling alkaline diets and early to bed routines. They contract rashes and inflammatory conditions easily. Most of these Fires suffer from heartburn, psoriasis or an itchy scalp.

The Fire lifestyle is an active one. Many advertisements promoting healthy lifestyles use Fire lives as examples to the rest of the world. They run on the beach, look fantastic and can save the drowning dog. Fire is fast, so there's a continual drive for improvement. Never let it rest says Fire, and even at home though it might be considered critical, it is Fires affection. They invented the phrase "if you rest, you rust".

In their relaxed moments Fire-Predominant people are often exhausted. They will play till they break then need urgent repair, but once repaired they'll say thanks and run out the door for more. Once they can control this tendency they enjoy a long, healthy life. They want the fastest best and biggest and then want the slowest, easiest and most comforting to recuperate. Warm, light atmospheres suit them in this situation.

Fire imparts greater sensitivity to sight, which means whenever you are looking around – the Fire constitution is awake. This also corresponds to the digestive Fire, so most problems associated with digestion are Fire problems. The sacred symbol for Fire is the triangle with the point facing upward, sharp and direct.

Famous Fire-predominant people include Napoleon, King Arthur, Hercules, Zena, Zorro, Superman, Batman, Batwoman.

Water Predominant.

Soft flesh, heavy bones, rounded shape.

Water people are the most caring. They symbolize protection, and humanity. Water people love others and nurse them, while being amazingly sympathetic. Water represents the power of compassion. It is Water that the Greeks referred to as the constitution that gives rise to life. Water occupies 90% of the surface of the planet. It has eroded the Grand Canyon, wearing things down rather than dominate them. Water always gets its way and it's more an evolution than a revolution, collusion rather than a force.

Water people are rarely driven to put the material aspects before human considerations. Even a person whose constitution is not primarily water, will put on weight if he develops a deeply humanitarian philosophy.

If it is time to deepen your human touch, to bring deeper loving values to your family, or to learn how to nurture and care for yourself, find a water person to guide you. By nature, Water people are patient, tolerant, peaceful, friendly and altruistic; also loyal, considerate and compassionate.

Globally the constitution water protects the innocent, defends the rights of children, protects and stops the forest from annihilation. Water creates corporate care and ethics programs and builds childcare facilities. It brings an ambulance when we need it and a doctor or nurse to help us when we are down. Water is universal bonding, a peace-loving constitution that will go to great lengths to protect the human aspect throughout.

You will find them in any business related to nurturing, caring, helping and compassion. Many nurses, chefs, careers are Water types. They love swimming and most water exercises.

Water people tend to overuse their water constitution in life and indulge greatly in Water food (carbohydrates, oils), too many Water emotions (hoarding, attachment), too many Water excuses (I am slow), and too many Water relationships (dependant). During imbalanced periods, Water people start putting on weight and accumulating fluids and fat in wrong areas of their body.

When any of us overdo our Water constitution, we gain weight, become sluggish, start feeling depressed, hopeless and insecure. It is easy for us at this stage to become dependent and clingy. Often when our water constitution goes into imbalance, we get addicted to food, especially the sweet variety.

Sometimes in the struggle to keep the promise "I will be always there for you" they forget about their own basic needs, and get dissatisfied with themselves. Slowly they build an extra fat layer to cover it up.

Another water challenge is boredom. This is usually covered up with extended sleep. Unfulfilled Water people resort to compensating their missing pleasure through eating. They often end up with water retention, swellings in the face, hands and feet. A further problem is their tendency to corpulence, which can lead to metabolic diseases such as diabetes.

Medically speaking, Water people have a weak circulatory system. Their adipose tissues need constant toning, their muscles can loose shape easily, pancreas may be over worked and lungs can be watery.

Water people go through the worst emotional shock when there's violence or cruelty around them. This pain can give them gout and high cholesterol, if prolonged. Even the strongest wrestlers – Water Predominant people – are not prone to immediate acts of violence.

The Water person, who chooses to stay in balance in his constitution, will surround himself with the following support.

1. Plenty of opportunity to care for others – to give and give care.

2. Family – Friends and family are the essence of Water people's life.

3. Movement and Exercise - low impact exercises and sports.

4. Love – lots of tenderness and feelings.

5. Respect for the real world issues of being on time (early for appointments) and predictability.

On a football field – one water player might rush in violently to defend his team mate or another might block a tackle or spin a ball rather than chuck it. Water people are like comrades, very friendly and supportive.

We associate love with this Water constitution. Whenever we feel it, Water is present. Add a bit of Fire to Water, you get the chemistry of romance. Water Predominant people bring a great deal of compassion to the world. Water Predominant people feel that the world is harsh and are always defending people, and their right to be passive. Those who stand for non-violence are using Water (need an abundance of this constitution) and once, priests and caregivers were strongly of the water constitution.

Often those involved in right-to-life issues are Water Predominant people. While their counterparts – AIR people argue for more choices, Water Predominant people meditate a lot. They love the passive connection and are drawn to such practices as Eastern Healing and well being.

Water Predominant people don't always make good business managers but do make great people careers like human resources and nursing. They are ideal in environments where people need to care about themselves and others. Water Predominant people bring fluidity to life circumstance, and love environments where people care.

Taste is a water function. No wonder we go in for tasty food when we need some comfort. The symbol that most represents the Water constitution is the circle, curves and oval shapes, smooth rounded and gentle.

Romantic, nostalgic people that they are, the waters gravitate to lakes and forests where there are smooth soft slopes and easy paths. When it comes to music, Water people love the violin, vocal harmony and lullabies.

Earth Predominant

Heavy frame, strong bones, solid muscles.

Security is a gift Earth people enjoy and this is felt through the roof over our heads, the money in our banks, the food on our tables, the clothes on our backs. Meeting obligations, making and keeping promises, being there when we need to be relied upon are the qualities of Earth constitutions.

Earth people are solid, realistic and highly structured. They are not easily moved by the wind or storms so they are the clear thinkers when there is trouble afoot. The Earth represents the capacity to make good what has been given to us all, our potential.

Earth constitutions hold the world in place. It is responsible for the laws, the rules. It is Earth that determines the forces that create matter, hold us in patterns and make life predictable and safe.

Earth Predominant people manage everything and organize others. If you are around an Earth person you may find yourself being organized. They tell you what is the most practical and time-tested method.

By nature, Earth Predominant people are strong, determined, friendly and caring also loyal, considerate, and dependable. They always love to talk about the history –'when I was a young lad...' They remember the milestones and civil wars and when the highway was built.

Earth people tend to overuse their Earth constitution. When this goes off balance, they complain – "they tell us what to do all the time". Once committed, an Earth person may fulfil his obligations at the cost of his life. Earth people are the most reliable among the five constitutions for punctuality and reliability in a material sense. This becomes their spiritual practice.

When any of us have an Earth imbalance, we become domineering, stoic and stubborn. We can become obsessed with others and this may look bossy.

Earth uses control as a form of affection and so, if you are around an Earth Predominant person you may find the control annoying but it is actually their way of giving love. They believe everything has a place and things should always be in those exact places. Anything sitting in a wrong place, like a book or pen, will drive them crazy. No wonder others call them control freaks!

If careless, overused Earth constitution in life can mean that Earth people slowly develop fibroid growths, enlarged organs, deposits in their blood vessels and ruptured arteries and organs. They can tolerate that kind of pain or suffering before they take any step. Their "Get on with it" attitude sometimes kills them.

Environmentally, Earth people are designed to live in any climate. They need food at regular intervals, while an organized lifestyle keeps them happy. Earth people thrive on real world physical work like building, gymnasiums or managerial work –they thrive in it.

Earth people are very trustworthy. They are true to their word and love others to be in integrity around them. Earth Predominant people are deeply hurt by the breaking of trust or commitment. This to them is sacred.

Solid environments suit the Earth Predominant persons. They are always very calculating and work out the fine details before proceeding with anything. They are meticulous in their ideas and very considered. Take a holiday with an Earth Predominant person and you will find that they have everything planned out. The strength of this is that little is left to chance.

Earth Predominant people love property investments. They feel a kinship with construction and building. They will hire a good team of people around them to get the job done but really when it all boils down, Earth is in control.

Because Earth Predominant people love order, they are attracted to shapes like squares and rectangles. The ancient Greeks built their buildings based on symmetry, proportion and order, a perfect motto for the Earth Predominant person. Everything fits into a mould for earth and so their ability to carry through any plan or idea is second to none. Once an Earth person gets their teeth into something, they'll rarely let it go until it's done (or dead).

The Earth person, who chooses to stay in balance in his constitution, will surround himself with the following support group.

1. Etheric visionaries and creative people to stimulate progress.

2. Space – strong furniture, oak and wooden floors.

3. Gymnasiums where strength and stamina can be sustained.

4. Protein rich food.

5. Respect for creativity, philosophy and the enjoyment of free thinking and exploration.

Formality comes easy for the Earth people. They dig the idea that one and one make two and therefore always want to know the order of things, what goes where and who's in charge of whom. Punctuality is their key, on time every time – consistency and predictability.

What antagonizes the Earth Predominant person most are unruly situations – such as those that Ether or Air Predominant people thrive in. When there is a lack of punctuality the Earth Predominant person takes this very personally and finds it disturbing to his peace of mind. Also resistance is a real bugbear for the Earth Predominant person. Described often as a very stubborn character constitution, Earth gets extremely agitated when there is resistance or stubbornness.

The environment and lifestyle that most upsets and antagonizes the Earth Predominant person is uncertainty, doubtfulness and complexity, summarized as chaotic. This pushes every Earth button and Earth people go to hell and back to try and remedy this chaos.

The most common positive feedback Earth Predominant people get is that they are kind-hearted, supportive and extremely practical. If you have an Earth person behind you, you can do almost anything. To a fine edge, Earth Predominant people can be relied on for all details.

Kind-heartedness is an earth quality. They will care for those they love and have taken responsibility for. It is often translated as controlling but at the end of the day this control is about saving time, money and energy. Whereas some constitutions learn by experience and waste a lot of precious earth time doing so, Earth tries everything to avoid such waste.

To this end, Earth types don't know when to let go. They hold and hold unable to sense the difference between support and interference. They always mean well. Earth people are tenacious and wonderful business and personal partners because you can trust them. This raises the challenge for Earth Predominant people because of their loyalty – sometimes they go outside the boundaries of contracts and relationships because they can't bring themselves to leave. Survival for them can become a double life.

Earth Predominant people are traditionalists. They treasure family and history and hold onto air looms for years and years. Their favourite colour is brown and their lifestyle can be best described as earthy, hands-on outdoor real world living. Don't cramp an Earth Predominant person indoors – that's a killer. Finally, you'll know the Earth Predominant person from one distinctive action, their handshake, a firm, big grasping friendly full hand grab.

Your Constitution At Work

Knowing your constitution at work means that if you are invited to do a certain task, you'll know how to do that task, your way. If you do it somebody else's way, they may be happy about it, but you won't be able to keep it up for long, it's not your way. For example a lady who was Water constitution was asked to manage an office of lawyers. She did a sincere job of it, but they complained daily. They sent her to training programs and all manners of training but she didn't change enough. She came to me stressed and broken. Her Water way of managing was not wrong nor could it be changed – it was just her way. Her company wanted something different. When she realized this, she left.

Really honouring diversity.

What we want to encourage is the evaluation of the Constitutions, so a Business can manage the unique characters of each individual within it, rather than expect generic responses to generic circumstances. We are driving away from value-based leadership toward a respect for individuality. Diversity means honouring uniqueness.

We need diversity within business. Cycles are nature's law. Everything changes from chaos to order, continuously. If the culture is Water based, stability will be the catch cry. If the culture is Fire based, most others in the business will burn out from constant change. The key is to know how to adapt, manage and live in fluctuating circumstances.

Organizational cultures are spiritually corrupt unless they account for all five constitutions. Cultures must flex. The Fire Predominant people – needed for change management and innovation must be able to thrive. The Water Predominant people looking after the humanitarian sides need space and Earth, Air and Ether must be welcomed. Corporate culture kills this freedom of spirit. These five constitutions must all have their offices in one place. This is truly the challenge of business life, but it's absolutely essential to great corporate performance that it works well.

To manage in your constitution is not to deny it. If you are Ether, there's no use in trying to quench that part of you because the company culture says, if it doesn't add up, it isn't worth talking about. An Ether Predominant person in that environment would absolutely guarantee misery.

Constitutional analysis is all about managing by constitution to bring out the best in everyone. So we create a culture of no culture. In an environment where diversity is the key, constitutions are respected and jobs, duties and tasks are allocated accordingly.

It goes further than this. Imagine a boardroom stacked with one constitutional type. Let's say, they are all Earth. Then as a board, due diligence will be extremely accurate. But then a tall, wide-eyed, etheric person comes in and starts celebrating the future possibilities of the business. The Earth Predominant people would collude and have him or her thrown off the board. The shareholders would love the Ether Predominant person because he was a visionary with big promises. The Board itself would then need to invent and justify the departure of the Ether member, probably the Chairperson, because they were absolutely out of their constitution in his presence.

We want to change this so we all recognize the constitution of each person in a blink of an eye. Then, well the Etheric Chair person could speak to the future, the Earthy board could speak to reality, and everyone would see that both are essential. This scenario is a real life case study in one of Australia's largest public corporations.

Belinda is a slim, tall woman with wide shoulders. She was working as a creative director for a private company. She had a window office with simple table and a set of drawers over against the wall. When the new management and changes came, she was given a more important office in a more congested area of the building where people could see, speak and connect with her as they needed. They thought this a good idea in order for the work to flow faster and more accurately. She started contracting all the seasonal bugs and her sleep was affected.

A Constitutional Analysis revealed she was an Ether predominant person who, after the changes, got frustrated with congested space and started losing energy and vitality. She spoke with her new bosses and went back to the limitless-sky-filled large window. Now life is back to normal.

David is a strong, broad shouldered stocky guy who loves his tennis. He's the company sales programmer responsible for managing all the 200 delivery trucks, their drivers and their sales.

In his office the walls are filled with charts and pins all over the place. The names of each route correspond with different areas and territories. His primary job is to manage the team, make sure they get their trucks filled with the right ice creams and that they are aware of any new point of sale deals the company is offering.

He was promoted and did such a great job at building sales that they put him in charge of Training and Development for the sales team. Immediately, David started putting on weight. His tennis suffered and he injured his knee. Twice he lost his temper in a Training Program and threatened one of the staff.

A Constitutional Analysis revealed David was an Earth predominant person who, after the changes, became extremely stressed at the unpredictability of his new job. He wrote a training manual, a monthly system was put in place, they hired a professional trainer and David went back to his old self.

Jenny was the General Manager for a public company. She was of medium height, rounded shoulders and what we call fleshy with a soft, rounded body. Her employment track record was a disaster. She had the final say in who was to be hired and nearly everyone she put on did not make it past the trial period.

When asked, Jenny said, "I really care for these people, I really want to give them a chance. Some people are really desperate and I want this company to give people a fair go."

Constitutional Analysis revealed that Jenny was a Water Predominant person. Her primary concern other peoples' wellbeing. Unfortunately, the jobs were stressful and demanding. Her choices were made on the wrong criteria. So she hired a Personnel consulting firm to manage the interviews and make the selections. The company has not looked back since.

In Constitutional Analysis: there is a simple philosophy: manage people to their constitution.

Summary

Ether - Vision, Inspiration

Air - Communication, Networking

Fire - Marketing and Sales

Water - Human Resources

Earth - Management – Finance

Ether at work.

Doing business with Ether Predominant types is a very special treat. Ether Predominant people are kind, gentle and love tranquillity, peace, freedom and stillness. They thrive when the world is calm and open. They honor wisdom and creativity in others and themselves. Cramp their style and you are sure to meet significant resistance. You have to give them lots of space to think and feel and contemplate the outcome. This may be frustrating because it feels like you are wasting your time with them. Ether Predominant people will delay making any business decision always looking for perfect and finally settling for less when they recognize that perfect is a theory and actuality has blemishes.

The strength of Ether in business is their deep thinking ideology. They are very open to new concepts and love a debate on anything theoretical. Sometimes nothing happens with Ether – it's all hypothetical but this is a vital ingredient of any business, in fact for some it's the key to success.

Ether guarantees that you are seeing the whole picture. Even to the point of distraction they will open every window, every door and every possibility until exhausted you finally understand that there were more angles to this venture than first met your eye.

Because of their big heart and this ability to think way outside the square, Ether Predominant people gravitate to careers where philosophy, charity, planning and conceptualising are emphasized. Often we label the Ether Predominant person the entrepreneurial spirit – the free-thinking big ideas person, but of course they need a team of doers in order to actually make anything happen in reality.

Ether Predominant people thrive where the climate is warm and bright, if it's too cool or too hot they melt or freeze into their cocoon and become unproductive.

When doing business with Ether don't be in a rush, it'll turn them off and they will not make good decisions under time pressure. Be friendly and open and avoid any form of confinement, strict rules and heavy approach. Ether Predominant people respond well to diversity, new ideas and questions like, "What do you think about that?"

You'll know when Ether Predominant people are engaged in the business, because they'll say "let's talk it over" or "I have a thought" or "I think we all ought to discuss this openly" – of course what they mean is "your ideas stink and I have a better one, which I forgot to mention in our earlier debrief and I thought of yesterday after 6 months of working on the project and it's probably going to change the direction of the whole businesses, but it's a good idea and I want to find an environment to mention it where you won't shoot me down for doing so". This is Ether's great skill – never stop creating – but unfortunately there's no off button.

Strangely with such a potentially antagonistic mindset of never ending ideas – it is judgment and criticism that is Ether's Achilles heel. They shut down and run when they feel that the environment they are in is judgmental or controlling. It's a managerial nightmare. Getting the best from Ether means openness yet, from a commercial viewpoint if the project keeps changing it'll never be built and certainly not on budget. Not only this, but the people around Ether go mad trying to put their finger on exactly what they are meant to be doing and what they should do with all the work they did on the last idea which this new idea replaced.

Ether Predominant people love gifts of books, music and anything to do with the philosophy of their passion. Mind you, they already spend half their spare cash on those things so be careful not to duplicate. They love the world of magic and spiritual concepts and always love to play games that involve "what if."

Anxiety is a warning sign, when Ether hits the stress wall, anxiety builds on anxiety to almost guarantee impractical and some times disastrous discussions that looked good in the short-term but have huge long-term ramifications. That's why Ether Predominant people need to manage their cool, they need lots of meditation, relaxation and things that alleviate stress (sometimes sex is the cure all). But if you are in business with an Ether person, and he is not adequately relaxed (sex) then, be warned – your life and your business are in jeopardy, the next thing they do might undo whole years of effort. Spirituality that involves peace and compassion favour the Ether Predominant person, calming music and spacious countryside retreats – lakeside or rainforest holiday homes are the perfect antidote to the stress of business life.

If Ether Predominant people become deactivated, unmotivated and depressed then the beach with rolling waves, fresh air and lots of walks in the cool evening are the key. Make sure they understand the difference between the antidote for excess (stress) and deficiency (lost motivation). Excess needs pacification so the green and tranquillity of lakes and countryside are the destinations. Deficiency is when the world has lost its charm and the thrill of being you has vaporized, work has become a drudge which is when Ether needs environments which uplift, stimulate and these are oceans, winds and starlit skies. By the way, if they are going to the beach, sun baking or extreme exercises in the hot sun are not advised. Excess sun and Ether are a bad mix, and a guarantee for skin problems, anxiety and disease.

Negotiations with Ether Predominant people take on a wondrous almost mystical feel. They love to trust and can't get past their uncertainties unless there's a good connection to the other party. Cross them and they become tyrants. The words Ether love to hear are: easygoing, new things, variety, take it easy, anything else, another way, and best of all, "what do you think – feel about that?"

Office environments that activate Ether are spacious, plain colours, silk, simple white and pastel. Calm music and open space activates the Ether in everyone. But it is Ether Predominant people who can live and work in these environments – long term.

Environments that pacify Ether – if they have gone to excess are green, watery, gentle and cushioned. To the extreme, if Ether is in stress mode they need Earth beneath their feet, solid thick timber, deep walls, security and strength from both the space and those around them. One has to know the signs. Ether of all the constitutions can swing quickly from excess to deficiency. The one environment will just not do. Ether needs options – the country home to pacify their stressed out overloaded self and the city home with space and open plan in order to stimulate their natural self into action. Some architects build multi-function spaces where rooms change within a house. In an office environment, Ether will walk around looking for a calming area, when their own office space (should be activating) becomes just too much.

It can be reflected in the cars they drive. An activating car will be a large four-wheel drive or something that says – “get away from it all, and I love space” but this will only do if there is not enough activation of the Ether constitution in the workday. Most Ether Predominant people love the warm cozy comfort of a luxury car: the warm seats, the smell of comfort and the smooth music playing in the quad speaker stereo. This is a car for the highly used Ether predominant person – looking to pacify themselves – a meditation on the move.

Ether Predominant people are symbolized in the animal world by the human mammalian: the Ape. More evolved than the animals they co-habit with, yet, in the wild it is only their brain that can guarantee their survival. Under equipped in the speed and armor departments – the human mammal relies on sensory skill and premeditated plans to outwit the rest of its species. Just like in the human mammalian species there are thousands of varieties – from smaller and faster to bigger and more powerful.

If Ether Predominant people are going to succeed in business, they need to embrace certain absolutes. The word itself conjures resistance in an Ether reader. But absolutes means that there are keys to success for Ether Predominant people in the business world, that make being Ether an absolute guaranteed winning edge. These keys are:

Focus on willpower – willpower is mind over matter, learning to concentrate on being in one place, mind, body and heart. Ether can drive the car, dream of next year's opportunity, talk on the mobile phone and carry on adjusting the car seat, all at the same time. It all seems to happen at once but to the observing passenger it feels like there is nobody at home, back seat drivers were invented to help Ether drivers remember when to turn left.

Goals – now for some of the other constitutions goals are natural. In fact as you'll see later for some constitutions we recommend that goals be dropped. But Ether, well – life can be lived in two ways: virtual reality and reality. It can be lived in your head or in actuality. Both are good, but if Ether has the ambition to create in the real world, not just dream and dream of how it could be, or should be, then, goals, timelines and deadlines that force their hand into decisions and conclusions are essential foods.

Discipline and schedules are foreign to Ether. Everything gets done eventually in the Ether world but the trouble is that life is ruled by other constitutions too. Other people need to interact with Ether, and those interactions demand some sort of predictability for both commercial and emotional comfort. So Ether needs to have sympathy for the worlds of others where time is a regular consideration, deadlines and profit are important and change is not always good.

Finally, as mentioned elsewhere in this book nutrition is the key for Ether Predominant people. Consistent meals, snacks, and a good regular diet regime with not too much variation will ground and support the beautiful free spirit and open hearted lifestyle of the Ether business person.

Air at work.

Amazing – that's the expression people use when doing business with Air Predominant people. How can you have so much happening, keep hold of the reins, have so many balls in the air and be so calm? While the rest of the world struggles with one or two tasks at the same time – air thrives on hundreds. The energy can be at best frenetic, but Air Predominant people love the multi-tasking approach. They love it when there are a hundred things happening at once even though they may complain "no one takes responsibility around here" but it's really impossible to take responsibility around an Air Predominant person. They want a finger in every pie and if it's not happening fast enough they'll have it done, completed, delivered and paid for before the office arrives for work next day.

Working with air is such a creative experience, the true lateral thinker, the hands on manager Air people are those leaders who in the movies have twenty assistants running behind them with mobile phones ringing at a frenetic pace even as the star signs autographs and is cool. No matter who you are, around an Air Predominant person in business, you always feel like he is going to step in and take over – it's like being an assistant rather than a team member.

The strength of air in business is this potent hands-on style. It is ideal in creative and unpredictable environments where customer service is unique or where design and creativity require constant input. Fashion and magazine management where opinion rather than fact determine the look and feel of the magazine requires air leadership because the leader has to be in 100 places at once, guaranteeing the look and feel is consistent.

Air Predominant people love the rhythm of life, movement of any sort is a joy for air, the challenge-response cycle is their bliss. So, Air Predominant people thrive around people especially where ideas and thoughts and concepts are being engaged and developed. Rather than philosophical in approach Air Predominant people are practical, they just love twenty ideas more than two.

The irony for air is their detachment. They may be thinking one thing one day and the complete opposite the next and they don't even blink. For air, ideas and thoughts are just variables, pawns on the chessboard and they are worthless apart from the stimulation in the quest for right answers.

What an exceptional ability! Being receptive to 100 different possibilities, no urgency to choose one, an ability to allow those ideas to co-exist and yet, productivity happens. Changeable you might ask. Air predominant people can change on a dime. They truly embrace diversity but never really let go of control, no matter how much an Air predominant person may say –"I want you to take responsibility for this" they never really let go. So, in the long-term, people just move to an organic style of interaction, nothing is concrete until the Air manager says so.

Another notable asset for Air – is the speed at which they learn. Talk about a sponge for information, Air can hear it one day and be teaching it the next. Their dexterity makes them ideal communicators – the constitutions who invented interactive leadership, the perfect teachers (can grow staff well because they are never far from the action.

Air is creative. Always innovating, holding hands and guiding people. If the staff is open to it, they'll learn so much and the result is exceptional. Air predominant people iterate solutions by working with those people who are at the coalface. Air Predominant people really make management a people experience.

However, be mindful that it can be demotivating for highly skilled and experienced people to be "interfered with" all the time. Air sees no problem with stepping across the lines of territory of possessiveness around whose work is whose. They just love the process, the cycles of think-do-work and so can't even imagine the possessive nature of those whose work has come to reflect a constitution of their personality. Air says – "Just change that a bit" – worker thinks – "I designed that all day yesterday". Air learned something and thinks, "we can improve that" and the worker invested their heart and soul into it. One is attached the other is not.

Because of this wonderful skill at multi-tasking, Air Predominant people gravitate to business areas that provide variety. Rather than manage a business, Air Predominant people manage projects – they prefer outcomes that can be seen and are variable, many projects rather than one business.

Air Predominant people are also prolific in the performing arts, dancers, artists and musicians, where skill and diversity create a dynamic complex yet team orientated environment.

Since air moves gracefully between situations they make great travellers, able to move here and there in a moment. Teachers and trainers whose life is orientated around being available for many people at once, different audiences every day – Air can sustain the demands.

Adaptable, continuously changing and innovative, Air Predominant people are determined. They hold onto the result, even if the process looks complex they are always committed to the outcome. Air thrives in warm sunny climates, but easily depletes and exhausts itself in windy and cold environments. Air Predominant people struggle in places where such extremes exist, like Canada – hot summers and frozen work performance.

Air is symbolic of the bird world. They are able to fly around to make good, taking seeds from place to place, collecting the food for their young and returning faithfully to nest. Birds fly south for the winter – unlike the bear – birds know that cold frozen and windy climates are no place for them to thrive.

Sometimes people call Air Predominant people air-heads. That means they appear scattered. But Air Predominant people are not scattered in their own mind, they just explore options and more options and alternatives and more alternatives. Air is about the dance – Air Predominant people are not scattered when it comes to the outcome, their approach instead of direct is to explore and touch a million points – but the result is never in question.

If you want to be on the right side of air in any negotiation or sales situation know that they love the following language: "Hey take it easy," or "tell me about it" (they love to share their thoughts verbally). Or "which one do you love?" Or "you are so adaptable". In business they'll sign the deal and on the way out the door be talking about the next deal or even changing the last one. If they buy a home, they are looking in the paper for another new home before they move in. Always looking for the options, always creative and always inspirational, Air Predominant people are the multi-skilled multi-faceted ones amongst us.

In closing a deal with an Air Predominant person, let them choose. If you narrow the options they may feel that there's only one choice. In your opinion there may be only one, but air loves the freedom to choose. Avoid lack in variety, my way or the highway is absolute guarantee of lost respect with Air Predominant people. They eventually talk themselves into their own right answer. Remember options and options, benefits and benefits and most important of all, learn to listen.

When it comes to surprises, Air Predominant people love them. They love special treats and when it comes to gift time, well it might be better to give them a gift voucher, what is great today may be worthless to them tomorrow. The first question Air Predominant people ask is where did you get it? What they actually mean is – "If I don't like it, which I do, but if I don't, can it be changed?" Without that information, Air Predominant people cannot embrace the moment fully.

Air Predominant people are built for speed and endurance. So if you go out at night with an Air Predominant person be careful for you may not get home till breakfast. They can dance all night but can't eat more than a mouthful before they are satisfied. So if you are planning an evening with an Air Predominant person – quality of food not quantity is the key and then entertainment and activity is their passion. If you are doing business with air – then join them in the dance, not too heavy on the facts, let them ask – give them time to talk themselves around, enjoy and keep it light until they are ready to dig in. Their questions will be so exact you'll be stunned at the accuracy. Like a bird circling above waiting for the right moment, Air will await and prepare before diving into the hard core of the days business.

The challenge in business for Air Predominant people is the impression they give the world that they are too vague, too airy and always fluctuate. It is not so really, but to the lion, the bird circling above the prey is wasting its time. Air Predominant people need to understand this about themselves so they are not drawn into the Fire too quickly so that criticism doesn't cause them emotional upset.

When you are around an Air Predominant person and they say "I am so confused" then you are witnessing the result of stress in their lives. Confusion is air's answer to excessive stress. This confusion can eventually lead to hyperactivity, instability and over changeability (no commitment).

Pushed even harder with more stress, and air begins to have panic attacks, fear can overwhelm them and their lives, mind and work environment can become cluttered and scattered. Nothing gets done.

Now, this is a big problem for Air. First they take on far more than any other constitution could consider in a day, and then – if they go into excess – i.e. they overdo their Air constitution – they turn their day into a knotted ball of string, huge amounts of activity but going around in circles. Even one such experience in an office can undermine authority of Air for the future.

Air needs lots of Earthy support and it has to be cut off where Earthy management can stop the spin and get the job done. An Air person often doesn't even know that he is stressed except for a little bit of isolation he may feel once the others withdraw. Earthy management can draw the line and air must be able to accept that at some point, ideas and options must give way to productive discipline and staff moral.

Now, if air is in excess the perfect space for air is amongst the green grass of home. A warm slowness, logs on the fire, a cozy comfy couch, strong arms and a plate of Earthy vegetables (even meat) will bring balance. Far away from digital and electronic devices, a log cabin in the middle of nowhere. No real effort – just a time to be still and let the mind calm. Yoga classes on a daily basis are good and plenty of water can help balance a spinning Air. Long warm (not too hot) baths and spa treatments with oils can also help calm the excess of air.

The ideal office to activate Air is busy open plan, where people can see and talk and share – but there must be variety – mixed temperaments, colourful walls and active phones. Air thrives on the variety of life. But in places where the energy is intense and frenetic, Air needs calm. Unpredictability is not good for Air, threatening or unsafe spaces are detrimental. If it all gets too much, Air Predominant people end up in the gymnasium at lunchtime preferably doing aerobics, fitness dance classes or on a tread mill for half and hour.

If Air people are not active in their work (deficiency) then living near flowing water, playing music and running long distances is great (their home can become a musical nightmare for the neighbours). Diving into music, photography and the arts is an Air bliss stream. But if Air is working to excess at work then stability at home is the key. Warm, sunny, windless places with lots of still water and smooth rhythm, predictable and safe, tranquil and at peace.

Fire at work.

If there's a need for a competitive culture, Fire is your constitution. They are ideal in these situations – they love a challenge. Even in a Yoga class, Fire Predominant people are looking around to see who they can compare themselves to. It makes for growth, fast change, transformation and drive.

> **"Sometimes people feel that whatever the work they are doing, it could not be what God intended for them. They blame the work. The missing piece here is not what is wrong with the work they are doing, but rather understanding the work they are performing right now in the context of their destiny."**
>
> Christopher Walker

Highly motivating Fire Predominant people can burn others out with their high energy and high expectations. They push and they push the goal in mind and sometimes the human cost and the nitty gritty details get left behind. Fire Predominant people are the keys to change, to getting through the tough times and to growth in the good times. If you are negotiating with a Fire Predominant person keep the energy alive and supportive. If things become slow and gentle and soft and spacious they'll switch off.

Language that Fire loves to hear is: precise, sharp, clear, picture this, powerful, intense, holiday and retire. This is energy, yet Fire knows the gift of calm relaxed lifestyles. Appeal to Fire by agreeing with them on their ideas that the world is too slow (they will spend a lot of money to help speed up progress). Therefore technology is a Fire birthday and they love time saving devices even if, after the fiddling about, there's potentially more potential for lost time.

In the office, Fire Predominant people like strong colour, vivid and sharp definitions, activated square shapes and lots of light. Energy in a Fire office is like the New York stock exchange and Fire Predominant people can do that job for a lifetime whereas most other constitutions would struggle in a week. When there is deficiency in Fire, in other words, there's nothing to compete with, Fire needs to activate this deficiency through exercise, action and direct application to task. Fire thrives in comparison so most biographies of inspirational people are read by Fire.

It needs mentors it respects and can grow to match and then another and another. Fire needs role models and mentors they can compete with.

If there are situations that need understanding, analysis and resolution Fire can do it best. They love the sprint, the physical middle distance: rowing and gymnastics, human against the constitutions sporting environments and therefore thrive in the marketplace.

If it's Christmas gifts you are looking for, remember Fire loves technology, faster and better (not bigger), things with luxury appeal and tools to make life more functional.

Be cautioned though, Fire in excess leads to aggression and violence. If there's not Fire and passion at work they bring it home with lots of expectations and energy. The wonderful domestic bliss they create with their big heart can turn sour if their Fire is not being consumed in the outside world of work and sport. Fire is always asking, "when will it happen?" or "when did it happen?" Time is life to Fire energy.

Stress for Fire results in illness. Acidity, joint problems kidney stones and blood pressure, Ulcers and tension can lead to many side affects even stroke and heart failure. Like in a pressure cooker, pressure can build and build while the internal components struggle with the overload.

Always prone to excess, Fire Predominant people can become ill, if there is too much of a good thing. The ideal balance for Fire during periods of excess is watery places. Places of tranquillity and calm, with soft trickling water, Zen gardens and warm baths. Fire Predominant people thrive in cool waterfront environments. They swing to excess and unhappiness in hot, damp places.

The animal of nature that best represents Fire is the lion. King of the jungle – or so it thinks, its pride and ego defend its domain. A voracious appetite, a ruthless capacity to do what must be done, stealthily and fast, the lion is in many ways the most vulnerable of animals in the jungle yet, in the right conditions – a powerful fighting machine.

If you are in business with Fire, celebrate the passion and purpose this constitution brings to your world, give them the lead on new development and take it back when the hard yards are crossed.

Keep the details out, look at the big picture and be sure not to step in their way. Pictures paint a thousand words for Fire, they can't wait for the slow people to catch up so be sure to have plenty of first aid on hand if you are working with them. Fire remains a wonderful spirited constitution that can transform and change any situation in the shortest possible time.

The keys to success for Fire Predominant people are: moderation, middle path, calmness of mind, and plenty of physical exercise.

Big hearted and caring, Fire Predominant people are always ready to help, you only need a gentle challenging gesture, glance or a word of request and they'll be on to it. They are also prone to burnout. Excessive play, work, demand, relaxation well, Fire people can become obsessed with anything.

Fire Predominant people are not the ideal ones to be in charge of your business. The reason is that Fire Predominant people are built for speed, for surging, challenging and continuous rigorous examination. They come with new ideas, new ways to do the same old thing. People just can't keep up with Fire management. Water, Earth, Ether and Air all struggle to sustain the pace. Not only that, the market is quite often unable to keep up with the changes. Business thrives, profit wise at least, on doing something repetitively. Fire would have no part of it, but the mantra would be to do it, change it, do it, and change it again. Like being permanently in transformation, Fire never stops innovating.

The strength of Fire is tenacity, intensity, analysis and creative application. Ideal where marketing is concerned or change analysis – where time is of the essence. Just do it, is a Fire energy slogan. Jump and see says Fire.

Water at work.

In business, nature and nurture are often in conflict and the motives for profit and wellbeing are sometimes challenging each other. Water represents wellbeing in true sense of the term. When you are working with Water constitutions: always put people first; that way you can be assured of their involvement and probably achieve the profit you desire.

The profound gift Water Predominant people bring to business is bonding. They connect people, nurture and build amazing loyalty. They are ideal maintenance managers, highly predictable and generous, the company and you will float along with many good employee feedback reports.

Water Predominant people want to know how what you are doing will affect people. They see performance and productivity from a human angle and love the ideals of compassion and humanity. Water Predominant people build flat company structures – trying to empower even the most challenged employees to happiness and reward.

If you are selling or negotiating with Water Predominant people, use the words: feel calm, peaceful, bathe, waves, and business ethics. In an office, Water Predominant people are activated by cooling colours, fluid designs, flexible objects (plants and lamp stands) circles ovals and smooth, soft fabrics.

If Water is being highly active at work, then the home may become almost slothful. Water can really let go when it needs to, creating a lifestyle akin to the couch potato. Books, television and fluids take the Water Predominant person to paradise and back but like all the constitutions too much can be detrimental. If the Water constitution is not activated at work then we find a very caring partner at home. Some would say smothering if done to excess. The Water Predominant person likes to be right and rarely stops before things happen the way they want.

Stress for Water means withdrawal. Now on the couch add a bowl of ice cream and some chips and Water people feel like they are on the inside and the world is on the outside. It's an easy existence for Water under stress, but this is incompatible with business success and achievement. Possessiveness, attachment and holding on are signs of a Water person gone into excess. Balance is required. Water Predominant people can become self-righteous, which means they are in serious overload, because Water people's last stand against collapse is to become self-righteous. Be careful with this indication of stress.

The perception many people have of this caring constitution is one of deeply attached and a worrier. This may, from time to time be the truth, but what is true caring other than attachment and concern. It is a matter of balance, anything done to excess can be smothering.

If you want to get on the good side of a Water Predominant person, speak these words, slowly: "Are you ok?" "Is this safe?" "It helps if ..."

When its time for a birthday gift, Water people love clothing, food and anything that makes life and the world for that matter – a safer place. Rarely do Water Predominant people enjoy being alone, with no one to care for it can be a nightmare for them. If it's a one person office, Water may find it hard, and if there are numbers and numbers then definitely Water Predominant people will find it a long-term struggle to stay healthy (not impossible – just not natural).

When Water Predominant people go to an extreme they put on weight. That in turn makes it hard for them to be active which means they put on more weight. That makes it harder to be active and the cycle goes on.

Water people are very proud. First it is a willingness to let go. When something isn't working, rescue just breeds desperation. When it's time to let go, it takes a lot of energy and courage (Fire) and Water people do have that within them. Further, they must acknowledge that a lot of the world cannot understand the feminine side to success and achievement. As a strong representative of compassion and peace Water people will often be accused of being too gentle or too kind or easily manipulated. That is the truth for Water; they are kind and vulnerable to manipulation but that is something they know and understand and their compassion guarantees that the world will get over it. Water Predominant people of all the constitutions must understand the process as being different and special, human and powerful. Water takes a long time to wear down rock, but because it stays consistent it does wear down and it always achieves its end.

Water easily suffers depression in cold and damp environments. You find that in Northern climates where the winters are long and dark, there are many Water Predominant people who suffer enormously. Once they would have migrated south because the environment dictated it, now they defy nature. Water Predominant people need to be compassionate with themselves first Water. Warm and dry is heaven for Water.

If work is not stimulating a Water person, they don't feel that they have enough opportunity to give care to people, then, it's vital they activate their Water constitution in their personal life. Taking a massage, stretching in a gentle yoga class, keeping the fluids up and joining people who have their hearts in the right place are typical Water. Being in nurturing environments with their partner, so they can both celebrate the beauty of the Water being.

Water people thrive in sporting environments involving swimming and steadiness like archery. Keeping the mind active through study and maintaining a healthy physical emphasis without emphasis on weight but more on healthy food, good air, cardiovascular exercise and lots and lots of love.

In a world where numbers and facts often dominate the business environment, Water Predominant people are like a breath of fresh air. Not always in alignment with maximum profit goals, they need to be mindful of the sort of culture they work in. And for those who employ Water people, they too need to be conscious that if they listen to Water – in the end they'll surrender profit for feeling good. It's the challenge the world has right now to find just this balance.

Water is always there to care, even if it costs them the job. Water constitutions believe people and their wellbeing come first. The Buddha was a Water guy.

Earth at work.

When the ancient gods built the Earth Predominant people, they did so because it was time to get something done, to actually make it happen. When it's loyalty, trust and reliability at stake in the material world, Earth has it all.

The Earth Predominant person is the manager, the one who, given a formula for success will ensure it will happen at any cost. They are the builders, the ones who manage the ideas thoughts and visions of the world and bring them to form. Yes, Earth is behind the Great Wall of China, the pyramids of Egypt, the great human made monuments to the powers of human will, Earth is the builder of dreams.

Beneath every great enterprise is Earth energy. The owners or entrepreneurs don't have to be Earth but they cannot live or survive or grow without Earth Predominant people. These are the people that ask how – rarely why.

In the business world stability, support reliability, grounding, establishment, firmness and solidarity are the call of the Earth energy. Earth Predominant people stick to a plan, and guarantee completion of any project or endeavour. On sports teams, they are the unflappable, the anchor, the link in the chain. You can always rely and put your trust in the hands of an Earth Predominant person.

So when negotiating with Earth keep in mind they love methodical, firm and on time commitments. They rely almost 100% on experience to prove anything and thrive when strategy is clear, a plan is set in concrete and integrity is made a strong core value.

In the office, Earth Predominant people love those brown leather lounges with the buttons stuck in, the fabrics are always rough and durable and the coffee table is 6 inches thick wood. Steel and metal beams can be exposed because it's a feeling of strength and reality and rectangular shapes for Earth are pleasing to the eye. Strong shoes, long lasting materials, and many antiques reveal the essence of Earth in an office.

Earth Predominant people love facts. "Cut to the chase now what are you trying to say?" may as well be their favourite line. Earth Predominant people often spark off Ether and Air who might very well lament the opportunities that aren't being pursued, rather than focus on the ones that are. While other constitutions worry about why and who, Earth people concentrate on when and where.

If Earth indulges in excesses, it can, like the other constitutions, turn strengths to weaknesses. Commitment can turn to absolute stubbornness, loyalty can turn to blindness, attention to detail can turn to time wasting retentiveness, and reliabilities can turn into stiff and frozen mindsets. Earth Predominant people are strict at the best of times – discipline is easy for them, but when stress takes Earth into excess, strict can become downright mean and stick to the knitting can become stubborn and obstructive.

Earth is the constitution of control. Ether may be the constitution of imagination, Air the constitution of possibilities, Fire the constitution of transition and Water the constitution of humanity. Earth is the constitution of control. What use would imagination, possibilities, transformation and humanity be, if there was no food on the table, if the electricity didn't flow to our homes or the water we drink was contaminated. What use would a business plan be without Earth to follow through with the details and implementation?

In the eyes of others, Earth can appear dominating and stubborn but this is a negative twist to a wonderful gift. However, Earth can, in spite of outer appearances take a lot to heart and when under extreme pressure or when out of control, develop very deep levels of low self-esteem. If this happens, Earth must seek support, otherwise their decisions in testing situations may lean toward an ego gratification rather than a healthy business logic.

For the Earth Predominant person who is not fully stimulated in their work, it is vital to activate the Earth constitution in their private life. Weight training is ideal, balanced with affirmations, investments, real estate development and stability in family matters.

When it's time to buy your Earth Predominant person a gift, consider that Earth Predominant people are essential people. Cosmetic life is no value to them. The gift must be real but functional. Useless paperweights will not survive the day they were presented.

If you need a bold, responsible, can-do-anything type of a leader you need not look beyond Earth. But if creative, variable, uncertain, no planning and totally unpredictable environments are essential for your success, then, those Earth Predominant people you work with should be kept well away from that ruckus. It will just not make for productive dynamics.

When it comes time to negotiate or sell to an Earth Predominant person, well it's very reasonable to use these words: Let's do it, let's manage that and let's stick to a plan. Earth loves anything that has solid routine, well-documented rules, provides a systematic plan, and is factual, methodical and repetitive.

The animal that most represents the Earth constitution are those that build. The elephant, strong and stable, the beaver focused and determined, the bull, strong and unstoppable, the hippopotamus – safe and guarded, the bear – storing things for winter and the dog, reliable, faithful and a friend for life.

By the way, if you are working with Earth Predominant people, never throw things out. Earth Predominant people store and store and store and store things. Just in case they are ever needed. They put things away, they file things they organize even the rubbish is well organized. Earth Predominant people hold on tight to the past, they value it, it provides security for them so be careful – those of you who are obsessed with letting go the past, Earth Predominant people have good cause to hang onto it, this is the Earth beneath their feet.

When it comes to climate – Earth Predominant people thrive in hot places. They can also cope extremely well in cold climates. So there are few places on the planet where this constitution cannot thrive, which is just as well, because they are the foundations beneath the building of cities and offices and businesses and forests. Without Earth Predominant people, we would all be living nomadic existences.

www.ingramcontent.com/pod-product-compliance
Ingram Content Group UK Ltd.
Pitfield, Milton Keynes, MK11 3LW, UK
UKHW022048190726
13855UKWH00002B/441